A BASIC REFERENCE
GRAMMAR OF SLOVENE

A BASIC REFERENCE GRAMMAR OF SLOVENE

WILLIAM W. DERBYSHIRE

Slavica Publishers, Inc.

Slavica publishes a wide variety of scholarly books and textbooks on the languages, peoples, literatures, cultures, folklore, history, etc. of the USSR and Eastern Europe. For a complete catalog of books and journals from Slavica, with prices and ordering information, write to:

Slavica Publishers, Inc.
PO Box 14388
Columbus, Ohio 43214

ISBN: 0-89357-236-5.

Printed in the United States of America.

This Work Is Dedicated To

RADO L. LENCEK

TABLE OF CONTENTS

Table of Contents   7

FOREWORD

The reference grammar which follows was written for speakers of English who are at the elementary through the intermediate levels of acquisition of the Slovene language. It attempts to present in a logical and easily comprehensible way the basic grammar of Slovene, beginning with a brief description of the Slovene language, its major dialects and its place among the Slavic languages. Then follows information on the alphabet, pronunciation and spelling rules. The major part of the work treats systematically and in a simplified form the major categories of speech: nouns, adjectives, pronouns, numeral declensions and verbal conjugations. Finally, there are brief sections treating prepositions, adverbs, information on a number of syntactic constructions relevant to the early stages of Slovene language study, word order and word formation.

The need for a work such as this one grew out of the author's own experience in studying Slovene. While there exist a number of grammars of the language for beginners, the majority of them published in Ljubljana, for the most part they neither present Slovene grammar in a systematic way, nor do they contain comprehensive charts of that language's grammar for easy reference in an appendix format. Furthermore, with few exceptions, available grammars are written exclusively in Slovene, requiring the learner to construct the grammar of Slovene as he or she progresses. It is the author's belief that employing the inductive method in the study of a Slavic language in most instances is not the most efficient path towards mastery. The latter is particularly true when applied to Slovene, which contains grammatical structures both more complex than many other Slavic languages (Russian, for example) and at the same time very different from languages such as English, Spanish or even German. The entire process can be accelerated and made more convenient with access to charts, lists and explanations

9

at one's fingertips.

In writing this text the author was guided and aided by extremely helpful hints from colleagues and was provided with examples by a number of native speakers of Slovene. He reminds the learner, however, that Slovene is a language which contains numerous allowable variant forms. A reference work of this scope cannot present every possible form and serves at best as a guide to the grammar as described by native linguists and grammarians. In those instances when the native informants did not agree on the correctness of a grammatical or lexical item, the author used as his final arbiter major comprehensive dictionaries and grammars published in Slovenia. The student is likewise advised to verify forms with a native speaker and to consult similar works should doubts arise when encountering an unexpected form.

This work constitutes a basic reference grammar of Slovene and has been written for use with any of the several existing grammars of Slovene*. The intended audience is an adult one possessing a command of the English language and a grasp of basic grammatical terminology as needed for the study of a Slavic language such as Slovene. Potential users may be university students, researchers in the Humanities, Social Sciences or Natural Sciences or those persons of Slovene descent who wish to improve their command of their ancestral tongue. Since this work describes the grammatical structure of the Slovene language, the author reminds the user that oral proficiency will be gained only through systematic work with speakers of Slovene.

This work would not have b een possible without the continuous support and encouragement of Rado L. Lencek of Columbia University, a true humanist, scholar and respected colleague. Prof. Lencek's dedication to his native Slovene language as well as to the fate of the other

* See bibliography at the end of the book.

"minor" Slavic languages has resulted, *inter alia*, in several roundtable discussions and scholarly panels sponsored by his university, the Society for Slovene Studies and the American Association for the Advancement of Slavic Studies and has served as the primary impetus for this author to codify the Slovene language in the form of a basic reference grammar.

Others who have shown a deep interest in, offered illustrative examples for and provided invaluable comments on this work include Marija Bolta, Henry R. Cooper, Jr., Ljuba Črnivec, Marc Greenberg, Irma Ožbalt and Joseph Paternost. To each of them I am deeply endebted.

The author wishes to express his sincere gratitude to the following agencies whose support enabled the completion of this work: The Department of Higher Education of the State of New Jersey, The Rutgers Research Council and The U.S. Department of Higher Education. Last, but not least, hearty thanks go to Dagmar Jensen who so patiently typed early drafts of the manuscript and to Mikhail Sakgobenzon and Bengt Erikson who provided gracious and much needed proofreadings of the manuscript and to the latter who drew the map on p. 13. The remaining and inevitable errors are the sole responsibility of the author who begs the reader's indulgence!

William W. Derbyshire
Somerset, NJ, and Seattle, WA, 1992

THE SLOVENE LANGUAGE

Modern Slovene is the official language of the Republic of Slovenia. The capital and largest city of Slovenia is Ljubljana, and its second largest city is Maribor. There are approximately two million speakers of Slovene in Slovenia, and large numbers of speakers of the language live in Slovene ethnic enclaves in neighboring Austria, Hungary and Italy. Many speakers of the language and persons of Slovene descent live throughout the world, including the English speaking world.

The language presented in grammars and taught in schools and universities is known as Contemporary Standard Slovene. It is the language of educated Slovenes and is used in all forms of artistic endeavor and in the mass media in Slovenia. Its speech area extends from the Julian Alps to the Croatian border not far from Zagreb and from the Hungarian border to the Italian littoral area. Slovene consists of many dialects with the major bases located in the following regions: Lower Carniola (Dolenjsko), Upper Carniola (Gorenjsko), Styria (Štajersko), the Pannonian region on the Hungarian border (Panonsko), Carinthia (Koroško), the Littoral along the Adriatic coast and the Italian-Friulian border (Primorsko) and the Rovte area (Rovtarsko) between the Littoral and Upper Carniola. The standard language is a composite of the dialects of the several regions of Slovene linguistic territory, but it is based primarily on the geographically central dialects of Dolenjsko and Gorenjsko.

Slovene is a member of the Slavic branch of the Indo-European family of languages. More specifically, it belongs to the South Slavic group of languages and is closely related to Serbo-Croatian and shares close affinities with the other South Slavic languages, Bulgarian and Macedonian. Additional sister Slavic languages include Russian, Ukrainian and Belorussian to the east and Polish, Czech, Slovak and Lusatian

12

to the northwest. As a member of the large
family of Indo-European group of languages, it
is related to English and German, as well as to
the Romance languages (French, Spanish, Italian,
et al.) and to many other languages which extend
from India to the British Isles and now to the
New World.

The map which follows is based on commonly accepted descriptions and shows a Slovene
linguistic territory which extends into Italy
and Austria to the west and north, Hungary to
the east and Croatia to the south.

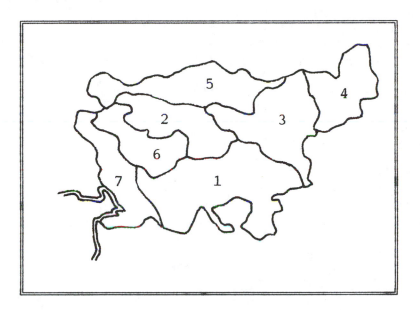

1. Lower Carniola (Dolenjsko)
2. Upper Carniola (Gorenjsko)
3. Styria (Štajersko)
4. Pannonia (Panonsko)
5. Carinthia (Koroško)
6. Rovte (Rovtarsko)
7. Littoral (Primorsko)

THE ALPHABET, SOUNDS AND SPELLING RULES

Slovene uses the Latin alphabet and employs 25 letters, three of which are used in combination with the diacritical mark ˇ. Presented below are the letters with the sound value for each.

Letter		Approximate sound value
A	a	(see notes below)
B	b	b as in bed
C	c	ts as in cats
Č	č	ch as in church
D	d	d as in day
E	e	(see notes below)
F	f	f as in face
G	g	g as in get (never g as in George)
H	h	h as in hit, but with stronger friction
I	i	(see notes below)
J	j	y as in yes (never j as in John)
K	k	k as in kite
L	l	(see notes below)
M	n	m as in man
N	n	n as in net
O	o	(see notes below)
P	p	p as in pet
R	r	(see notes below)
S	s	s as in set
Š	š	sh as in shop
T	t	t as in ten
U	u	(see notes below)
V	v	(see notes below)
Z	z	z as in zigzag
Ž	ž	zh as s in the word pleasure

The following letters appear in foreign words:
    Q q (listed after P in dictionaries)
    W w (listed after V in dictionaries)
    X x (listed after W in dictionaries)
    Y y (listed after X in dictionaries)

Letters above which represent consonant sounds in Slovene are:

> *b, c, č, d, f, g, h, j, k, l,*
> *m, n, p, r, s, š, t, v, z, ž*

Letters above which represent vowel sounds in Slovene are:

> *a, e, i, o, u*

NOTES ON THE CONSONANT SOUNDS L, R AND V:

1. The letter **l** represents two basic sounds:
   (a) Before vowels and the consonant **j**, **l** is similar to the **l** in the word lumber, e.g. **líst** 'leaf' and **ljudjé** 'people'.
   (b) Before all other consonants and at the end of words, **l** is normally pronounced as **w** in way or now, e.g. **vólk** [vówk] 'wolf' and **cél** [céw] 'whole'.
   There are a number of exceptions to (b) above which must be learned individually. They include certain literary words as well as some foreign borrowings, e.g. the words **glágol** 'verb', **kultúra** 'culture' and names such as **Ciríl** and **Báltimore** in which **l** retains the pronunciation noted in (a) above.

2. The letter **r** represents a rolled sound made by vibrating the tip of the tongue near the back of the upper tooth ridge. A similar sound does not exist in most varieties of English, but it is found in languages such as Spanish, Italian or Russian. When **r** occurs at the beginning of a word before another consonant or between two consonants it is pronounced with the vowel [ə] preceding it (see note on the vowel **e** below), for example in the words **rdèč** [ərdèč] and **vŕt** [vért].

3. The letter **v**, like **l**, represents two basic sounds:
   (a) Before vowels it is pronounced like **v** as in very, e.g. **víno** 'wine' and **povédati** 'to tell'.

(b) At the end of words and before consonants, it is normally pronounced as **w**, e.g. **pràv** [pràw] 'just' / 'quite' and **pévka** [péwka] '(female) singer'.
Again, like l, there are some exceptions to (b) above which must be learned individually.

NOTES ON VOWELS

Stressed vowels in Slovene may be short or long, while unstressed vowels are short. In two instances the long vowels may be open or closed. It is not possible to find exact English equivalents for all the various vowel sounds in Slovene, and the comments which follow provide only a broad indication of their sound value. When learning Slovene, the student should imitate carefully the pronunciation of vowels by native speakers and avoid any tendency to diphthongize them.

[**Note**: the use of accent marks already appears in examples above, and a description of them follows in the section below entitled "accent marks".]

Long and short a/i/u: The preceding vowels may be short or long when stressed and, as noted, short when unstressed.

	short	long
a as in father	bràt 'brother'	máti 'mother'
i as in beet	sìt 'full'	sín 'son'
u as in moon	krùh 'bread'	múha 'fly'

e/o: These two vowels may also be short or long when stressed. Further, when long, they may be open or closed. Without the stress they are both short and open. Each is discussed separately below.

Long open o: Its pronunciation lies approximately between the **a** in **all** and the **o** in **mode** as in the word **vôda** 'water'.

Long closed o: Its pronunciation lies approximately between the o in mode and the oo in mood as in the word nós 'nose'.

Short o: Its pronunciation is similar to the a in the word all as in the word otròk 'child'.

Long open e: Its pronunciation lies approximately between the e in bet and the a in bat, but longer in duration, as in the word têle 'calf'.

Long closed e: Its pronunciation lies approximately between the e in let and the a of late, but longer in duration, as in the word léto 'summer'.

Short e: Its pronunciation is similar to the e in bet as in the word èn 'one'.

The vowel [ə]: The letter e may also represent a short vowel with a pronunciation similar to the a in the word above. In dictionaries and grammars the symbol ə is often used to indicate when e is pronounced as [ə], but in standard texts it is normally spelled e. It may occur under stress as in the word pès [pəs] 'dog'. Unstressed it is found frequently in the final syllable of words, e.g. in the word véter [vétər] 'wind'.

Those instances when e is pronounced as [ə] are not dealt with in detail in this text, although a number of examples are drawn to the reader's attention. The learner will come to predict its occurence with some confidence over time. (See also the note on r above.)

[Note: The learner may hear in the pronunciation of some educated native speakers of Slovene the vowel i instead of e before the consonant r, e.g. cérkev [církəw] and Prešéren [prešírən].

       For those learners whose primary goal is to achieve a reading knowledge of Slovene, vowel

quality (ˆ vs. ´) and quantity (ˆ, ´ vs.ˋ) - see
the section entitled "accent marks" below - will
not be a major concern. For the learner wishing
to acquire a knowledge of the spoken language,
particular attention must be paid from the very
beginning to the pronunciation of one's instruc-
tor, recordings or native speakers. Failure to
distinguish between short and long vowels or
between open and closed o and e, for example,
can easily lead to misunderstandings. Notice the
difference in the meanings in the pairs of words
which follow:

kònj (short o)	nominative sing.	'horse'
kónj (long o)	genitive plural	'horse'
péti (long closed e)	infinitive	'to sing'
pêti (long open e)	numeral	'fifth'
nósi (long closed o)	'(he/she)	'carries'
nôsi (long open o)	imperative	'carry!'

ACCENT MARKS

As noted above, grammars and dictionaries of Slovene employ the following diacritical
marks over vowel letters: ´, ˆ and ˋ to
designate quantity (short vs. long) and quality (open vs. closed). The mark ´ (acute accent)
is used to designate the long stressed vowels
a, e, i, o and u, while the mark ˋ (grave accent)
is used to designate the short stressed vowels
a, e, i, o and u. The mark ˆ (circumflex) indicates that the quality of long stressed e or o
is open, as opposed to the closed quality of a
long stressed e or o (marked by ´). Thus, all
vowels in Slovene may be short or long, with the
exception of ə, normally written as e, which is
always short. Accent marks are not used in standard texts. They will, however, be used throughout this work in order to increase the learner's
awareness both of the place of stress and of
vowel quality and quantity.

PLACE OF STRESS

Slovene has free stress, i.e. it may fall on any syllable of a word. Furthermore, once established, the place of stress may be non-mobile, i.e. it remains on the same vowel in all forms of those words which change endings by form, or it may be mobile, i.e. it moves between different forms within a word. The latter case, however, occurs with less frequency, since there is a tendency for stress to be non-mobile in Slovene. It is common in linguistic descriptions of Slovene to designate a non-mobile stress which falls on the root of a word and remains there in all forms, e.g. in nouns and verbs, as an **A** stress pattern. An example is the noun **léto** 'summer'(see p. 26). Words in which the stress is non-mobile and falls on the ending in all forms, e.g. the present tense of the verb **govoríti** 'to speak', are said to have a **B** stress pattern. Words in which the stress is mobile, i.e. moves ahead or back in specific and pre-dictable forms, as in the noun **srcè** 'heart' (see p. 26) are said to have a **C** stress pattern.

Likewise the quality of a vowel may alternate between open and closed in different forms of the same word, e.g. in the noun **móst** 'bridge' (see p. 26).

[Hint: Not every word in Slovene receives stress, e.g. prepositions, auxiliary verbs and short forms of pronouns do not. It will help the learner to remember that in accented words which have a long vowel (´ or ^), that vowel auto-matically receives the stress. In an accented word without a long vowel, the stress is short (`) and normally falls on the final syllable.]

PAIRS OF VOICED AND VOICELESS CONSONANTS

Consonants in Slovene are considered to be voiced or voiceless. Some of them, those listed below, form pairs and undergo assimila-tion, i.e. they change their character under

specific conditions, a fact not reflected in
spelling. In such pairs the presence of a paired
voiceless consonant immediately before a paired
voiced consonant requires its voicing. Paired
voiced consonants which occur before paired
voiceless consonants or at the end of a word are
pronounced like their voiceless counterparts:

Voiced	Voiceless
b	p
d	t
g	k
z	s
ž	š
[dž] (as j in jam	č
[dz] (as dz in adze)	c
(Also voiceless are f and h.)	

SOME EXAMPLES:

	Written	Pronounced	
b > p	hríb	[hríp]	'hill'
	golóbček	[golópčək]	'little dove'
p > b	lép dán	[léb dán]	'beautiful day'
d > t	mlád	[mlát]	'young'
	odhòd	[othòt]	'departure'
t > d	svátba	[svádba]	'wedding'
g > k	snég	[snék]	'snow'
k > g	kdó	[gdó]	'who'
z > s	vóz	[vós]	'car'
	izpít	[ispít]	'test'
ž > š	móž	[móš]	'husband'
	težkó	[teškó]	'difficult'
š > ž	vaš déd	[važ dét]	'your grandfather'

CONSONANT ALTERNATIONS

In certain inflectional and derivational
categories of Slovene a series of consonant
alternations will occur automatically. This will
be seen in the former, for example, in certain
verb forms, specific case forms of nouns, the
formation of comparative adjectives and in the

latter in the area of word formation. The most common alternations are:

k, t and c	~	č
g, z and zd	~	ž
h and s	~	š
sk and st	~	šč
d	~	j
r	~	rj
l	~	lj
n	~	nj

SOME EXAMPLES:

okó	'eye'	oči	'eyes'
krátek	'short'	kračína	'shortness'
drág	'expensive'	dráži	'more expensive'
rézati	'to cut'	réži	'cut!'
tíh	'quiet'	tíšji	'quieter'
pisáti	'to write'	píšem	'I write'
iskáti	'to seek'	iščem	'I seek'
prepustíti	'to yield'	prepuščen	'yielded'
mlád	'young'	mlájši	'younger'
oráti	'to plow'	órjem	'I plow'
dáleč	'far'	dálje	'farther'
tánek	'thin'	tánjši	'thinner'

NOTES ON CONSONANT ALTERNATIONS

1. The consonant alternations below are less frequently encountered. They are used primarily in the conjugation of a limited number of verbs, in creating certain types of imperfective verbs (see p. 93 for examples) and in forming past passive participles (p. 87).

sl~ šlj   posláti ~ póšljem
            'to send' ~ 'I send'

p ~ plj   kápati ~ káplje
            'to drip'~ 'it drips'

b ~ blj   ljubíti ~ ljúbljen
            'to love' ~ 'loved'

v ~ vlj   slavíti ~ slávljen
            'to glorify' ~ 'glorified'

m ~ mlj   dremáti ~ drémljem
            'to doze' ~ 'I doze'

2. In verbs whose infinitive ends in -či the root contains a -k or -g, and these alternate respectively with -c and -z in the imperative form only:

	'to say'	'to lie down'
Infinitive	rêči	léči
1st person sing.	rêčem	léžem
Participle in -l	rékel	légel
Imperative	rêci(te)	lézi(te)

3. The r ~ rj alternation is limited and less predictable and occurs in certain forms of nouns, adjectives and verbs. For examples see p. 29.

SPECIAL NOTE ON THE ALTERNATION OF O WITH E

In masculine and neuter noun declensions (for example, in the instrumental singular, the dative plural and genitive plural) and in adjective declensions (see p. 39) an expected o after the consonants č, š, ž, c and j, which are considered soft consonants in Slovene, is spelled and pronounced as -e.

Compare: *z ávtom*   *'by car'*
          z ênim udárcem   *'with one strike'*
                  and
          bélo víno   *'white wine'*
          rdéče víno   *'red wine'*

THE GRAMMAR OF SLOVENE

Slovene is a language in which nouns, pronouns, adjectives and numerals are declined, i.e. they change form by case. Verbs are conjugated, i.e. they change form by person and number, and they also denote tense (e.g. present, past, future). Words which do not change form by case include adverbs, conjunctions, particles, interjections and prepositions, the last of which, however, determine case selection for declined words.

The descriptions which follow will serve as a basic reference for nouns, adjectives, pronouns, numerals, verbs, adverbs and prepositions. The information presented in this text should be sufficient to guide persons undertaking a study of Slovene through the elementary and intermediate levels of that language. A number of exceptions are included in this description, i.e. irregularities likely to be encountered at the elementary and intermediate levels of Slovene language study. This reference material does not claim to be complete or exhaustive, but every effort has been made to include those exceptional forms needed realistically at the early stages of Slovene language study.

NOUNS

Nouns in Slovene are characterized by **gender**, **case** and **number**. There are three genders: **masculine**, **feminine** and **neuter**. Further, nouns are declined, i.e. their form changes by case through the addition of sets of **endings** the choice of which depends on the function of the noun within a given sentence. There are six cases: **nominative**, **accusative**, **genitive**, **dative**, **locative**, and **instrumental**. The numbers are **singular**, **dual** and **plural**.

GENDER

In the nominative case, the dictionary entry form, most masculine nouns end in a consonant. Feminine nouns end in -**a** or, in some cases, in a consonant. Neuter nouns end in -**o** or -**e**. The case forms (sets of endings) for masculine and neuter nouns are identical in most cases, and they constitute **CLASS I** for nouns.

Feminine nouns which end in -**a**, together with a limited number ending in a consonant, form **CLASS II**. All other feminine nouns ending in a consonant form **CLASS III**.

There is a small number of nouns which do not decline.

CASE

As noted above, the selection and use of cases in Slovene is determined by the function of the noun within the sentence:

The **NOMINATIVE** case is the basic form of the noun, and its primary function is to serve as the subject of a sentence.

The **ACCUSATIVE** case, *inter alia*, corresponds to the direct object in English. It is also governed by (i.e. its use is required by the presence of) numerous verbs, and it is used with certain prepositions. In the case of masculine singular nouns only, the choice of endings depends on whether the object being referred to is animate or inanimate. If it is animate, i.e. refers to a person or animal, the ending is identical to the genitive case. The accusative ending for inanimate masculine objects coincides with the nominative case. (See pp. 103-104 for additional information on the topic of animate vs. inanimate.)

The **GENITIVE** case fulfills a wide variety of functions, one of which is to indicate possession. It is also used after many prepositions, after numerals, and it is governed by certain verbs. (Information on additional uses of the genitive is found on pp. 105-107).

The **DATIVE** case is the equivalent of the indirect object in English, i.e. a person or object acting as the recipient of the action of specific verbs. It is also used with a number of prepositions.

The **LOCATIVE** case is used with a number of prepositions which denote certain concepts of location and time.

The **INSTRUMENTAL** case is used with a number of prepositions which denote certain concepts of space and means and functions.

NUMBER

The **SINGULAR** number is used when discussing one subject or object.

The **DUAL** is employed only when referring to two counted subjects or objects. (See pp. 102-103 for additional information on the use of the dual in Slovene.)

The **PLURAL** is used when referring to more than two subjects or objects.

Note: There is a limited but significant number of nouns in Slovene which occur in the singular or plural only, e.g. **zlató** 'gold' for the former and **vráta** 'door' for the latter. Such words often refer to things which are not countable, e.g. **zràk** 'air'.

ENDINGS

Words which end in a consonant may be said to have a **zero ending**. (# is a linguistic symbol which is often used to designate a zero ending.) Typically, nouns change form by adding an ending to the **root** or **stem** consonant, the final consonant of a word before its ending. Nouns which end in a vowel (-a, -o, or -e) drop that vowel and replace it with the proper ending. Note the final root consonant in the following words: *móst#, lét-o, kníg-a, stvár#*.

Further, the number of different case endings in the singular does not exceed four, since some endings serve for more than one case. In the plural there may be six different endings, and in the dual the nominative and accusative coincide, as do the dative and instrumental. The genitive and locative cases of the dual coincide with the same cases of the plural.

SAMPLES OF DECLENSIONS

CLASS I	MASCULINE AND NEUTER NOUNS

singular

	'traveller'	'bridge'	'year'	'heart'
N	pótnik	móst	léto	srcé
A	pótnika	móst	léto	srcé
G	pótnika	mostú/mósta	léta	srcá
D	pótniku	môstu	létu	sŕcu
L	pótniku	môstu	létu	sŕcu
I	pótnikom	móstom	létom	sŕcem

dual

	'traveller'	'bridge'	'year'	'heart'
N/A	pótnika	mostóva	léti	sŕci
D/I	pótnikoma	mostóvoma	létoma	sŕcema

plural

	'traveller'	'bridge'	'year'	'heart'
N	pótniki	mostóvi	léta	sŕca
A	pótnike	mostóve	léta	sŕca
G	pótnikov	mostóv	lét	sŕc
D	pótnikom	mostóvom	létom	sŕcem
L	pótnikih	mostóvih	létih	sŕcih
I	pótniki	mostóvi	léti	sŕci

CLASS II	FEMININE NOUNS

singular

	'book'	'mountain'	'church'
N	knjíga	gôra	cérkev
A	knjígo	gôró	cérkev
G	knjíge	gôré	cérkve
D	knjígi	gôri	cérkvi
L	knjígi	gôri	cérkví
I	knjígo	gôró	cérkvijo

dual

N/A	knjígi	gôri	cérkvi
D/I	knjígama	gôráma	cérkvama

plural

N	knjíge	gôré	cérkve
A	knjíge	gôré	cérkve
G	knjíg	gôr/gorá	cérkev/cerkvá
D	knjígam	gôràm	cérkvam
L	knjígah	gôràh	cérkvah
I	knjígami	gôrámi	cérkvami

CLASS III   FEMININE NOUNS

singular

	'thing'	'thought'
N	stvár	mísel
A	stvár	mísel
G	stvarí	mísli
D	stvári	mísli
L	stvári	mísli
I	stvarjó	míslijo

dual

N/A	stvarí	mísli
D/I	stvaréma	míslima

plural

N	stvarí	mísli
A	stvarí	mísli
G	stvarí	mísli
D	stvarém	míslim
L	stvaréh	míslih
I	stvarmí	míslimi

Note: The presence of alternative forms for a
single case indicates that either form is acceptable. Such double forms may differ in place
of stress, e.g. in the locative singular of
cérkev, or in the choice of case ending, e.g.
the genitive plural of gôra and cérkev above or
the genitive singular mostú/mósta on the preceding page. While either form may be encountered,
it is emphasized that the individual speaker
will always use one or the other systematically.
Throughout this work many such double forms will
be presented. In most cases the first form given
will be the one more preferred in current standard usage, while the second form may be either
more literary, dated, colloquial or dialectal in
nature. The declension of the word gôra, for
example, indicates the possibility of a non-
mobile A stress pattern on the first syllable or
a mobile C stress pattern shifting to the ending
in several forms. As noted earlier there is a
growing tendency in Slovene to prefer a non-
mobile stress. Those forms are more common
today, so that in this instance gôra stressed on
the o of the root throughout is to be preferred.

MISCELLANEOUS COMMENTS

1. Many masculine and feminine nouns have a so-
   called "fleeting" vowel in their stem, i.e.
   the final vowel letter (-e- or -a-)is dropped
   throughout the declension: cérkev ~ cérkve
   'church', dán ~ dné 'day', pès ~ psà 'dog',
   and stárec ~ stárca 'old man', véter ~ vétra
   'wind'.Belonging to this group are most nouns
   ending in -ec, -eg, -ek, -er and -ev in which
   the vowel -e- is pronounced [ə]. (See also
   note under e on p. 17.)

2. (a) All borrowings, except those which end in
   -a, are considered to be masculine, i.e. no
   borrowings become neuter nouns in Slovene.
   They are declined like Class I nouns, e.g.
   finále 'finale', kíno 'movies',rádio 'radio',
   táksi 'taxi'. (See also note 1. (b) below.)

(b) Borrowings which end in -a are feminine and are declined like Class II nouns. (See also note 1 on p. 33) Those borrowings which refer to a female but do not end in -a, however, are not declined, e.g. lady [lé(j)di], madám and proper names such as Ingrid and Nancy.

NOTES TO NOUN DECLENSIONS

MASCULINE AND NEUTER (CLASS I) NOUNS

1. (a) Many masculine nouns ending in -r add -j- throughout their declension (see consonant alternations, p. 21), e.g. dóktor ~ dóktorja, the nominative and genitive/accusative cases of the word 'doctor'. Other words in common use include:

    cár 'tsar', kúhar 'cook', papír 'paper'

The rule, however, is limited, and many nouns in common use ending in -r do not add a -j-. Among them are found:

bór	'pine'	góvor	'speech'
dár	'gift'	séver	'north'
dvór	'court'	Máribor	(city name)

Nouns with a "fleeting" vowel (see 1. above) do not add a -j, so that, for example, names of months ending in -er, e.g. septêmber 'September', do not add -j-, but those ending in -ar do, e.g. fébruar 'February'.

(b) The -j- is also added to foreign borrowings ending in a vowel, e.g. táksi ~ táksija 'taxi' and komité ~ komitéja 'committee'. These nouns are masculine.

2. Nouns ending in -e which designate masculine beings as well as a few neuter nouns add the suffix -et- in all declined forms, while some other neuter nouns add the suffixes -en- or -es- throughout their declensions:

(a) The suffix -et- occurs in the word ôče ~ očéta, the nominative and genitive/accusative

cases of the word for 'father'. The same suffix occurs in a few proper names, e.g. Jóže
~ Jóžeta 'Joseph' and the masculine noun
fantè fantéta 'boy', as well as in the
following neuter nouns:

déte	~	déteta	'baby'
deklè	~	dekléta	'girl'
têle	~	teléta	'calf'

(b) The suffix -es- occurs in a group of
commonly used neuter nouns ending in -ó
(see 10.(c) below also):

drevó	~	drevésa	'tree'
koló	~	kolésa	'wheel'
nebó	~	nebésa	'sky'
peró	~	perésa	'pen'
teló	~	telésa	'body'

(c) The suffix -en- occurs in a few commonly
used neuter nouns ending in -me:

imé	~	iména	'name'
vrême	~	vreména	'weather'

3. A small number of monosyllabic Class I masculine nouns in common use take an optional
   stressed -ú ending in the genitive singular,
   e.g. dár ~ darú/dára 'gift'. Others include:

glás	'voice'	móst	'bridge'
grád	'castle	nós	'nose'
lás	'hair'	sád	'fruit'
léd	'ice'	sín	'son'
lés	'wood'	stráh	'fear'
méd	'honey'	zíd	'wall'
mír	'peace'		

4. A relatively large group of monosyllabic
   Class I masculine nouns are like móst and add
   the suffix -ov- in the dual and plural (see
   the declension of móst on p. 26). Among the
   most frequently encountered are:

brég	'shore'	móst	'bridge'	tók	'current'
cvét	'flower'	nós	'nose'	vál	'wave'
dár	'gift'	pás	'belt'	véter	'wind'
dólg	'debt'	pláz	'avalanche'	vólk	'wolf'

dóm	'house'	plód	'fruit'	vóz	'car'
dúh	'spirit'	réd	'order'	vrát	'neck'
glás	'voice'	sín	'son'	vŕh	'peak'
gód	'name day'	stráh	'fear'	vŕt	'garden'
grád	'castle'	svét	'world'	zíd	'wall'
lés	'wood'	tát	'thief'	zvón	'bell'

5. (a) A few masculine nouns take the ending -jé instead of -i in the nominative plural:

  lás ~ lasjé   'hair'
  móž ~ možjé   'man'
  zób ~ zobjé   'tooth'
  člôvek ~ ljudjé   'person'

  (b) A number of other masculine nouns may take either -je or -i in the nominative plural, including:

  bràt ~ brátje/bráti   'brother'
  déd ~ dédje/dédi   'grandfather'
  gospód ~ gospódje/gospódi   'sir/Mr.'
  študènt ~ študéntje/študénti   'student'

6. The normal ending for the genitive dual/plural of masculine nouns is -ov. A few masculine nouns, however, take a zero (#) ending (note the change in vowel quantity between the nominative singular of kónj and otròk):

  kónj 'horse'   otrók 'child'
  lás 'hair'   vóz   'car'
  móž 'man'   zób   'tooth'

The genitive plural of člôvek (nominative plural ljudjé) 'person' is ljudí (see 10.(a) below).

7. The dative plural for some masculine nouns is -ém instead of -om:

  lás   ~ lasém   'hair'
  ljudjé ~ ljudém   'people'
  móž   ~ možém   'man'
  zób   ~ zobém   'tooth'

8. The normal locative dual/plural ending for masculine and neuter nouns is -ih. A few nouns, however, take the ending -éh, including:

drvà ~ drvéh	'firewood'
lás ~ laséh	'hair'
ljudjé ~ ljudéh	'people'
móž ~ možéh	'man'
tlà ~ tléh	'floor'
zób ~ zobéh	'tooth'

9. The normal ending for the instrumental plural
   of masculine and neuter nouns is -i, while a
   few nouns take the ending -mi:

drvà ~ drvmí	'firewood'
lás ~ lasmí	'hair'
ljudjé ~ ljudmí	'people'
móž ~ možmí	'man'
tlà ~ tlémi/tlí	'floor'
zób ~ zobmí	'tooth'

10. A number of nouns in common use display
    changes in the stress or form of their stems:

    (a) Forms in the singular for the word
    člôvek 'person' display a stress shift but
    are otherwise regular:
        človéka, človéku, človékom.
    Its dual forms are: človéka, človékoma.
    Its nominative plural is ljudjé (see also
    notes 5.(a), 6., 7., 8. and 9. above)

    (b) Forms in the singular for the word otròk
    'child' are otrôka, otrôku, otrôkom.
    Its dual forms are: otróka, otrókoma.
    Its nominative plural is otrôci, and the
    other forms are otrôke, otrók, otrôkom,
    otrócih, otróki.

    (c) The following two neuter nouns add an
    -es suffix and have a consonant alternation
    throughout their declensions:
        uhó ~ ušésa 'ear'
        okó ~ očésa 'eye'
    [Note: The plural of okó is očí. It is de-
    clined like stvár, i.e it becomes a feminine
    noun. See p. 27.]

11. The noun **dan** 'day' is declined as follows:

singular	dual	plural
N *dán*	*dnéva*	*dnévi*
A *dán*	*dní/dnéva*	*dní/dnéve*
G *dné/dnéva*	*dní*	*dní*
D *dnévu*	*dnévoma*	*dném/dnévom*
L *dné/dnévu*	*dnéh/dnévih*	*dnéh/dnévih*
I *dném/dnévom*	*dnéma/dnévoma*	*dnémi/dnévi*

FEMININE (CLASS II) NOUNS

1. Borrowed nouns ending in -a are declined like Class II feminine nouns, e.g. **fúnkcija** 'function'.

2. The normal genitive plural ending for nouns in Class II is zero (#), but a small number may be found with the ending -**á**, e.g.
    gôra ~ gôr/gorá 'mountain'
    sêstra ~ sêster/sestrá 'sister'
and one in -**í**: **beséda ~ beséd/besedí** 'word'.

3. The noun **gospá** 'madam'/'Mrs.' has exceptional endings:
-**é**   in the dative/locative singular and in
            the nominative/accusative dual/plural
-**á**   in the genitive dual/plural
-**éma** in the dative/instrumental dual
in the plural -**ém** (dative), -**éh** (locative),
        -**émi** (instrumental)

4. The feminine nouns of Class II which end in a consonant almost always have the ending -ev. Also included here are the nouns
    máti 'mother' and **hčí** 'daughter'
(the genitive being **mátere** and **hčére**, the accusative **máter**, **hčér** and the instrumental **máterjo**, **hčérjo**).

5. To feminine nouns of Class II ending in -a belong a number of masculine nouns, e.g. **slúga** 'servant', **koléga** 'colleague' and **vójvoda** 'duke'. They are grammatically feminine (i.e.

they decline like feminine nouns), but their
modifiers are always masculine and decline as
masculine modifiers, e.g. 'our man-servant':
                nominative   genitive
             nàš slúga   **nášega slúge**
Despite the preceding rule, it is noted that
there is a growing tendency to decline these
nouns as masculine nouns of Class I. In the
sentence which follows the genitive singular
of the word **koléga** occurs as **koléga** instead
of the expected **kolége**:

>   *Môjega koléga ni túkaj.*
>   'My colleague isn't here.'

(See pp. 105 and 121-122 for an explanation
on the use of the genitive in sentences of
this type.)

FEMININE (CLASS III) NOUNS

        A comparison of the declensions for the
nouns **mísel** and **stvár** on p. 27 reveals a different set of endings for the instrumental singular, the dative and the instrumental dual, and
the dative, locative and instrumental plural for
those nouns which take the stress on the ending
(mostly monosyllabic ones such as **kóst** 'bone'):
        -ijo, -ima, -im, -ih, -imi (unstressed)
                as opposed to
        -jó, -éma, -ém, -éh, -mí (stressed)
        Further, there is a small group of nouns
like **mísel** which have the ending -jo in the
instrumental singular, -ma in the dative and
instrumental dual, and -mi in the instrumental
plural, e.g. **mìš** 'mouse'.

NOTES FOR STRESS ON NOUNS

1. As noted earlier (see p. 19), nouns may have
   a non-mobile stress, i.e. the place of stress
   remains on the same syllable throughout the
   declension. Many masculine nouns have an A
   stress pattern on the root, such as in the
   word **pótnik** on p. 26. A small group of nouns

displays a B pattern with the stress on the
ending, e.g. **stebèr** [stəbə̀r] 'pillar'. A
limited number of nouns, including some words
in frequent usage, take a C stress pattern in
which the stress moves from the root to the
ending in the genitive singular and in all
dual and plural forms, e.g. **móst** (p. 26).

2. The vast majority of neuter nouns display an
   A stress pattern, e.g. **léto** (p. 26). A few
   nouns have a B stress pattern, e.g. **sencè**
   'temple'. In those neuter nouns with a C
   stress pattern the nominative and genitive
   singular endings are stressed, while on the
   remaining forms the stress moves to the root
   of the word, e.g. **srcé** (p. 26).

3. In a large number of words, including both
   masculine and neuter nouns, a variant of the
   A stress pattern is seen in which the place
   of stress moves within the stem so that it
   always falls on the penultimate (next to the
   last) syllable, e.g. **jêzik ~ jezíka** 'language',
   têle ~ teléta 'calf'. Others include:

bôžič	'Christmas'	**prêdlog**	'proposal'
člôvek	'person'	**prôstor**	'space'
jêlen	'deer'	**rázred**	'classroom'
Jêrnej	(proper name)	**sósed**	'neighbor'
mêdved	'bear'	**zákon**	'law'
ôtok	'island'	**závod**	'institution'

4. The vast majority of feminine nouns ending in
   -a display an A stress pattern, e.g. **knjíga**
   (pp. 26-27). In a small group of nouns in
   which the -e- of the stem represents the
   vowel [ə] there is an optional B stress
   pattern, e.g. e.g. **stèza/stezà** 'path'. There
   is a group of nouns in common use with an
   optional C stress pattern moving from the
   stem to the ending in the following cases:
   accusative, genitive and instrumental singular, dative and instrumental dual, all cases
   of the plural, e.g. **gôra** (see note on p. 28
   with reference to **gôra**).

5. Feminine nouns of Class II ending in a consonant do not display a B or C stress pattern,
   i.e. the stress is a non-mobile A pattern remaining on the stem, e.g. cérkev (but note
   possible variants in stress and form for the
   preceding word on p. 28).

6. Some feminine nouns of Class III may have an
   A stress pattern throughout the declension,
   as in mísel (p. 27), while the others display
   a C stress which moves to the ending in the
   genitive and instrumental singular and in all
   forms of the dual and plural, e.g. stvár (see
   p. 27 and comments on Class III nouns on
   p. 34).

ADJECTIVES

Adjectives in Slovene, like nouns, distinguish gender, case and number. They are declined and have sets of endings, and they reflect the gender, case and number of the noun which they modify . For masculine adjectives in the nominative singular, there is the possibility of distinguishing between the indefinite ('a'/'an') and the definite ('the') forms. With the exception of the nominative and accusative cases, in the singular masculine and neuter adjective declensions coincide. In the singular feminine adjectives have endings like the noun **knjíga** (see pp. 26-27). In the dual, there is an opposition of masculine to feminine and neuter for the nominative-accusative case only. In the plural, forms for four of the six cases are identical for all three genders.

Adjectives in Slovene have three degrees: **positive, comparative** and **superlative.** Each is fully declined.

The vast majority of adjectives in Slovene are declined like **bogàt** 'rich' which follows:

MASCULINE /	NEUTER	FEMININE

singular

N	*bogàt/bogáti*	*bogáto*	*bogáta*
A	*N/G*	*bogáto*	*bogáto*
G		*bogátega*	*bogáte*
D		*bogátemu*	*bogáti*
L		*bogátem*	*bogáti*
I		*bogátim*	*bogáto*

dual

N/A	*bogáta*	*bogáti*	*bogáti*
D/I		‹ *bogátima* ›	

37

plural

N	*bogáti*		*bogáta*		*bogáte*
A	*bogáte*		*bogáta*		*bogáte*
G		<	*bogátih*	>	
D		<	*bogátim*	>	
L		<	*bogátih*	>	
I		<	*bogátimi*	>	

NOTES TO ADJECTIVE DECLENSIONS

1. The definite form of the adjective is made by adding the ending -i to the indefinite masculine adjective as in **bogàt člôvek** 'a rich man' vs. **bogáti člôvek** 'the rich man'. Appropriate questions eliciting the indefinite or definite form include the words **kákšen** and **katéri**:

    Kákšen člôvek? 'What kind of a person?'
      Bogàt člôvek.
    Katéri člôvek? 'Which person?'
      Bogáti člôvek.

2. (a) Adjectives ending in -ski, -ški, -ji, -nji cannot be used in the masculine nominative singular without -i:

        slovénski   'Slovene'
        angléški   'English'
        dívji   'wild'
        srédnji   'middle'

(b) Adjectives which are derived from nouns and indicate possession and are formed with the suffixes -ov/-ev or -in are inherently definite and do not require the definite form ending -i in the masculine nominative singular, e.g. **očétov** 'father's', **máterin** 'mother's'

(c) In certain instances the use of the definite form is obligatory, e.g. with ordinal numerals **péti dán** 'the fifth day', after demonstrative **tísti sméšni člôvek** 'that funny man', with comparative adjectives **mlájši bràt** 'younger brother' and in phrases in which the adjective qualifies the meaning of a modified

noun such as in **béli krùh** 'white bread' or
sádni vŕt 'orchard'.

3. (a) One adjective, **májhen** 'small', has special
   definite forms for all three genders:
        máli, mála, málo.

   (b) The adjective **vêlik** 'big' also has forms
   for the definite which are distinguished by
   vowel quality and a stress shift in all three
   genders:
        Indef. **vêlik, velíka, velíko**
        Def.   **véliki, vélika, véliko**

   (c) Two adjectives display a shift in stress
   in the masculine forms: **dêbel ~ debéli** 'fat',
   rôjen ~ rojéni 'born'.

4. Adjectives whose stems end in -c, -č, -ž, -š
   and -j end in -e in the neuter nominative and
   accusative rather than the expected -o, e.g.
   domáče 'domestic'. (See comment p. 22.)

5. Many adjectives, particularly those ending in
   a simple -k, -n, -r or -l, have an -a- or an
   unstressed -e- [=ə] present in the masculine
   nominative singular form. These are fleeting
   vowels which drop in all other forms of the
   adjectival declension, e.g.
        težák(or **têžek**) ~ **têžki, têžka, têžko**
             'difficult'
        tájen ~ tájni, tájna, tájno 'secret
        dôber ~ dôbri, dôbra, dôbro 'good'
        tópel ~ tópli, tópla, tóplo 'warm'

6. A number of adjectives are not declined. Some
   display gender only, e.g. **ràd, ráda, rádo**
   (plural: **rádi, ráde, ráda**) 'glad' (for the
   special use of **ràd** see p. 111), while a number of adjectives of foreign origin display
   neither gender nor are they declined, e.g.
   šík 'stylish', **fájn** 'fine', **gáy** [géj] 'gay',
   béž 'beige', **príma** 'top rate', e.g. **príma
   hotél** 'a top rate/swell/first class hotel'.

The latter are quite popular, but only some are accepted in the literary language.

NOTES ON STRESS FOR ADJECTIVES

The vast majority of Slovene adjectives have an A stress pattern (non-mobile on the stem), i.e. **bogàt** (see above). A small group of adjectives may have a B stress pattern (non-mobile on the ending in all forms), e.g. **temèn, temnegà**, etc. 'dark', but it is often an optional stress. The tendency is towards the A stress pattern for all adjectives. One finds, for example, the adjective **temèn** in the variant forms **temán** and **tèmen**. The latter form is the preferred one, and the stress falls on the first syllable where it so remains throughout its declension. **Note:** The vowel in the root of this adjective is [ə].

THE COMPARATIVE DEGREE

The comparative degree of adjectives in Slovene is formed by the simple addition of one of the following suffixes: -š-, -j- or -éjš- to the root. The resulting forms are fully declined like adjectives in the positive degree (see notes for selection of suffix). Alternatively there exists a compound form employing the words **bòlj** 'more' or **mànj** 'less' before the positive degree of participles and those adjectives ending in -ji, -ov, -in, -ski and -ški, e.g. **bòlj razbít** 'more broken', **mànj urejèn** 'less orderly'. With either of the preceding formations, comparisons in Slovene are made by using the preposition **od** followed by the genitive case or the words **kòt, kàkor** or **ko** (the latter being more colloquial) followed by the nominative case:

> **Péter je mlájši od Bórisa.**
> 'Peter is younger than Boris.'
> **Vésna je staréjša kòt (sem) jàz.**
> 'Vesna is older than I (am).'
> **Jánez ní takó stàr kàkor (si) tí.**
> 'Janez is not as old as you (are).'

THE SUPERLATIVE DEGREE

The superlative degree of adjectives in Slovene is formed by the simple addition of the stressed prefix nàj- to the comparative degree: nàjlepši (= nàj- + -lep- + -š- + -i) 'prettiest' or by the use of the compounds nàjbolj 'most' or nàjmanj 'least',e.g. nàjbolj ohránjen 'the best preserved'. In constructions such as the following either preposition **od** or **izmed** followed by the genitive case may be used: Dúšan je od/izmed vseh nàjmočnejši.'Dušan is the strongest of all.'

NOTES FOR FORMING THE SIMPLE COMPARATIVE

1. The suffix -š- occurs with monosyllabic stems ending in -b, -p and -d. The final -d of the stem undergoes an alternation before the addition of the suffix -š-. (See Consonant Alternations, p. 20.)

lép	*'pretty'*	*lépši*	*'prettier'*
slàb	*'weak'*	*slábši*	*'weaker'*
húd	*'bad'*	*hújši*	*'worse'*
mlád	*'young'*	*mlájši*	*'younger'*
ràd	*'glad'*	*rájši*	*'gladder'*

In some cases the final consonant of the stem is lost before the addition of the suffix -š-:
   gŕd ~ gŕši 'ugly' ~ 'uglier'
   tŕd ~ tŕši 'hard' ~ 'harder'.

2. Adjectives which end in -ek, -ak or -ok drop that suffix, and the final consonant of the stem alternates.

globòk	*'deep'*	*glóblji*	*'deeper'*
krátek	*'short'*	*kráčji*	*'shorter'*
nízek	*'low'*	*nížji*	*'lower'*
ózek	*'narrow'*	*óžji*	*'narrower'*
širòk	*'wide'*	*šírši*	*'wider'*
sládek	*'sweet'*	*slájši*	*'sweeter'*
tánek	*'thin'*	*tánjši*	*'thinner'*
težák	*'heavy'*	*téžji*	*'heavier'*
visòk	*'tall'*	*víšji*	*'taller'*

3. The suffix -j- occurs with monosyllabic stems
   ending in -g, -k and -h. Consonant alternations take place.

blág	'mild'	blážji	'milder'
drág	'dear'	drážji	'dearer'
tíh	'quiet'	tíšji	'quieter'

4. The suffix -éjš- occurs with all other adjectives and is always stressed.

bíster	'clear'	bistréjši	'clearer'
bogàt	'rich'	bogatéjši	'richer'
číst	'clean'	čistéjši	'cleaner'
míl	'gentle'	miléjši	'gentler'
močán	'strong'	močnéjši	'stronger'
nòv	'new'	novéjši	'newer'
stár	'old'	staréjši	'older'

5. The following adjectives have irregular
   comparatives:

blížnji	'near'	blížji	'nearer'
dóber	'good'	bóljši	'better'
dólg	'far'	dáljši	'farther'
láhek	'easy'	lážji	'easier'
májhen/máli	'small'	mánjši	'smaller'
vêlik	'big'	véčji	'bigger'

6. A number of adjectives have alternate forms
   for the comparative. Some of those listed
   below are not in current use and may be found
   only in older literature or in dialects.

globòk	'deep'	glóblji or globóčji
		or globokéjši
krátek	'short'	kráčji or krájši
mêhek	'soft'	méčji or mehkéjši
širòk	'wider'	šírši or šírji

7. In addition to forming comparatives by using
   the suffixes -š-, -j- and -éjš-, the positive
   form of an adjective may be prefixed by pre-
   giving the meaning 'too' or 'extremely':

   | predólg | 'too long' |
   | prelép | 'extremely pretty' |

8. The construction čim....tem.... is used with
   the comparative degree of adjectives (as well
   as with adverbs) in the following way:

   čim véčji, tem bóljši
      'the bigger the better'
   čim pametnéjši, tem bòlj zahtéven
      'the wiser the more exacting'
   čim préj, tem bólje
      'the sooner the better'
   čim bòlj zgódaj, tem bólje
      'the earlier the better'

ADVERBS

Adverbs in Slovene modify verbs, adjectives and other adverbs. They may come at the beginning, in the middle or at the end of a phrase or sentence. Adverbs are not declined and supply information about:

time	kdáj	'when'	védno	'always
degree	zeló	'very'	samó	'only'
manner	takó	'so'	skúpaj	'together'
place	kjé	'where'	túkaj	'here'
amounts	kóliko	'how much'		

Others pose **questions** such as zakáj 'why' or **causal relationships** such as zató 'therefore'.

Those adverbs which can occupy a relative position in a sentence have special relative forms (see also note 3. on p. 52):

Kám gréš?
'Where are you going?'
Pójdi, kámor hóčeš!
'Go where you want!'
Kóliko denárja imáte?
'How much money do you have?'
Kólikor vém, očéta ní domá.
'As far as I know father isn't home.'

Certain adverbs use the particle **le** for emphasis. When the particle follows the word it is written together with it. When **le** precedes it is separated by a dash, e.g. tàm + le > tàmle 'there'!, tjàle 'there'! (motion), tùle 'here'!, takóle 'so'!, as opposed to le + tù > le-tù 'here'!, le-tàm 'there'! (see note 5. on p. 53).

In addition to the adverbs provided above, adverbs derived from adjectives in Slovene are extremely common, e.g. tájno 'secretly' from tájen 'secret' and prijázno 'kindly' from prijázen 'kind'. Adverbs derived from adjectives usually coincide with the neuter nominative singular form ending in -o or -e. Sometimes the -o is stressed in the adverb form, e.g. lepó 'beautifully', as opposed to the unstressed -o preferred for adjectives: lépo.

Like adjectives, adverbs derived from them may appear in the **positive**, **comparative** and **superlative** degrees. Refer to pp. 41-43 for their

44

formation. See also note 7. on p. 42 for the use
of the prefix **pre-**.

    lepó   lépše   nájlepše
'beautifully/more beautifully/most beautifully'

      Listed below are commonly encountered
adverbs which display consonant alternations or
exceptional forms in the comparative. Many of
the corresponding adjectives are on pp. 36-38.

      The learner will notice that in a large
number of cases there exist alternate forms with
abbreviated suffixes so that, for example, both
blíže and **blížje**, **húje** and **hújše** or **méče**,
méčje, **mehkéje** or **mehkéjše**, may all be encountered. Native speakers of Slovene will often
prefer one form over another, and some of the
forms are found only in literary texts. The list
below presents the shorter of the variant forms
(shortest when applicable):

blízu	'near'	*blíže*	'nearer'
čésto	'often'	*čésče*	'more often'
dólgo	'long (time)'	*dálj*	'longer'
dôbro	'well'	*bólje*	'better'
drágo	'costly'	*dráže*	'more costly'
globôko	'deeply'	*glóblje*	'more deeply'
hudó	'badly'	*húje*	'worse'
kasnó	'late'	*kasnéje*	'later'
krátko	'briefly'	*krájše*	'more briefly'
lahkó	'easily'	*láže*	'more easily'
málo	'little'/'few'	*mànj*	'less'
mehkó	'softly'	*méče*	'more softly'
nízko	'low'	*níže*	'lower'
širôko	'widely'	*šírše*	'more widely'
tího	'quietly'	*tíše*	'more quietly'
velíko	'a lot'/'much'	*véč*	'more'
visôko	'highly'	*víše*	'more highly'

      In addition to being derived from adjec-
tives, a number of adverbs in Slovene are formed
from other parts of speech.

examples
from pronouns:
      zakáj, **čemú** 'why', 'what for'
      (both derived from **káj** 'what')

from nouns:

dánes	'today'	from	dán	'day'
nocój	'tonight'	from	nóč	'night'
jútri	'tomorrow'	from	jútro	'morning'

from verbs:

ponevédoma   'unknowingly'
   from védeti   'to know'
gledé   'in view of'
   from glédati 'to look at'

PRONOUNS

Pronouns in Slovene are fully declined. They are traditionally divided into the following categories: **personal, interrogative, indefinite, possessive, demonstrative** and **relative**. The most important ones are presented here.

Personal pronouns have stressed and unstressed forms (clitics). Stressed forms are used to indicate emphasis. Additional information on clitics is found in the chapter on word order. In the spoken and written language personal pronouns in the nominative case are normally omitted except for emphasis or to avoid confusion of person in ambiguous verbal forms, e.g. the conditional. Declensions of personal pronouns are given below. Acceptable alternate forms are those listed as "or", while the clitic forms are preceded by a slash (/). Forms with two stresses indicate that either stress may be found.

singular

	'I'	'you'	[reflexive]
N	jàz	tí	_____
A	mêne/me	têbe/te	sêbe/se
G	mêne/me	têbe/te	sêbe/se
D	mêni/mi	têbi/ti	sêbe/si
L	mêni	têbi	sêbi
I	menój	tebój	sebój
	or	or	or
	máno	tábo	sábo

	'he' 'it'	'she'
N	òn ônó	ôna
A	njêga/ga	njó/jo
G	njêga/ga	njé/je
D	njêmu/mu	njéj or njì/ji
L	njêm	njéj or njì
I	njím	njó

47

dual

	'we two'		'you two'	
	(m/n)	(f)	(m/n)	(f)
N	mídva	mídve	vídva	vídve
A/G		náju		váju
D		náma		váma
L		náju		váju
I		náma		váma

'they two'

	(m)	(n)	(f)
N	ônádva	ônidve	ônidve
A/G		njú or njíju/ju or jih	
D		njíma/jima	
L		njíju/njìh	
I		njíma	

plural

	'we'		'you'	
	(m/n)	(f)	(m/n)	(f)
N	mí	mé	ví	vé
A		nàs		vàs
G		nàs		vàs
D		nàm		vàm
L		nàs		vàs
I		námi		vámi

'they'

	(m)	(n)	(f)
N	ôní	ôná	ôné
A		njé/jih	
G		njìh/jih	
D		njìm/jim	
L		njìh	
I		njìmi	

[**Note**: Short forms of the accusative case are
always combined and written together with monosyllabic prepositions, and the stress falls on
the preposition, e.g. **záme** 'for me' (as opposed
to the emphatic **za mêne**), **prédte** 'before you',
pódnjo '(moving) under it'. Compare the latter
form with the instrumental case **pod njó** '(rest-
ing) under it'. Further, there is a special con-
traction for the masculine and neuter accusative.
It is **-nj** (as opposed to the enclitic form **ga**)
seen in **nánj** 'onto it' (cf. **na njêga**).]

INTERROGATIVE (followed by relative form)

	'who'		*'what'*	
N	*kdó*	*(kdór)*	*káj*	*(kár)*
A	*kóga*	*(kógar)*	*káj*	*(kár)*
G	*kóga*	*(kógar)*	*čésa*	*(čésar)*
D	*kómu*	*(kómur)*	*čému*	*(čémur)*
L	*kóm*	*(kómer)*	*čém*	*(čémer)*
I	*kóm*	*(kómer)*	*čím*	*(čímer)*

Other Pronouns

(m)	(n)	(f)

1. The following are possessive pronouns:

(m)	(n)	(f)	
svój	*svôje*	*svôja*	*'one's own'*
mój	*môje*	*môja*	*'my'/'mine'*
tvój	*tvôje*	*tvôja*	*'your/s'*
njegóv	*njegóvo*	*njegóva*	*'his'*
njén	*njéno*	*njéna*	*'her/s'*
nájin	*nájino*	*nájina*	*'our/s(two)'*
vájin	*vájino*	*vájina*	*'your/s'(two)*
njún	*njúno*	*njúna*	*'their/s'(two)*
naš	*náše*	*náša*	*'our/s'*
vàš	*váše*	*váša*	*'your/s'*
njíhov	*njíhovo*	*njíhova*	*'their/s'*

2. Demonstrative pronouns:

(m)	(n)	(f)	
tá	*tó*	*tá*	*'this'*
tísti	*tísto*	*tísta*	*'that'*
óni	*óno*	*óna*	*'that'(distant)*
ísti	*ísto*	*ísta*	*'same'*

ták	táko	táka	'such'
tákšen	tákšno	tákšna	'such a'
tólik	tóliko	tólika	'so much'
tólikšen	tólikšno	tólikšna	'(as) much (as)'

3. The following list contains a number of the most commonly used interrogative, relative and indefinite pronouns:

čigáv	čigávo	čigáva	'whose'
drúg	drúgo	drúga	'other'
kàk	káko	káka	'some'/'any'
kàkšen	kàkšno	kàkšna	'any kind of'
kákšen	kákšno	kákšna	'what kind of'
katéri	katéro	katéra	'which'/'whose'
kólik	kóliko	kólika	'how large'
kólikšen	kólikšno	kólikšna	'(as) large (as)'
néki	néko	néka	'a certain'
nobên	nobêno	nobêna	'none at all'
sám	sámo	sáma	'alone'
vès	vsè	vsà	'all'
vsák	vsáko	vsáka	'every'

The pronouns in 1., 2 and 3. above are fully declined, differing in detail from the adjectival declensions found on p. 37. Note the declensions of **tá** 'this' and **vès** 'all':

singular

	(m)	(n)	(f)		(m)	(n)	(f)
N	tá	tó	tá		vès	vsè	vsà
A	N/G	N	tó		N/G	N	vsó
G	téga		té		vsegà		vsè
D	tému		téj/tì		vsemù		vsèj/vsì
L	tém		téj/tì		vsèm		vsèj/vsì
I	tém		tó		vsèm		vsó

dual

	(m)	(n)	(f)		(m)	(n)	(f)
N/A	tá	té/tì	té/tì		vsà	vsì	vsì
D/I	téma				vsèma		

plural

N	*tí*	*tá*	*té*	*vsì*	*vsà*	*vsì*
A	*té*	*tá*	*té*	*vsè*	*vsà*	*vsè*
G		*téh*			*vsèh*	
D		*tém*			*vsèm*	
L		*téh*			*vsèh*	
I		*témi*			*vsèmi*	

NOTES ON PRONOUNS

1. Standard grammars are not consistent in their presentation of the dual forms for personal pronouns. The nominative case of the dual is listed in the charts above as **mídva / mídve**, **vídva / vídve** and **ônádva / ônidve**. One may also encounter the following variant forms for the nominative case of the feminine: **médve / védve / onédve**. Similarly, not all grammars agree on allowable forms for the locative of the dual. In addition to those listed in the chart, one may also also find the forms:

         náma   **váma**   **njíma**

2. (a) Indefinite pronouns also include:
        nihčè (gen. nikógar)   'nobody'
        nìč   (gen. ničésar)   'nothing'
        nobêden   'not one'
   (See p. 105 for information concerning the use of double negatives.)

   (b) The prefixes **malo-, marsi-, ne-, ni-** and **vsak-** may be added to a number of pronouns (as well as to adverbs) such as **kdó, káj, kàk, kàkšen** and **katéri** producing words with indefinite meanings, e.g.
        nékdo   'somebody'
        níkdo   'nobody'
        vsákdo   'everybody'
        málokdo   'hardly anyone'
        màrsikdo   'many a person'
        nékaj   'something'
        málokaj   'hardly anything'
        màrsikaj   'many a thing'

3. Relative pronouns(and adverbs) in Slovene are
   formed by adding the suffix -r(-) to the root
   of pronouns and are fully declined. (See, for
   example, the declensions of kdór and kár on
   p. 43.) Included among relative pronouns are
   the words kákršen 'like', kólikršen 'such as'
   and čígar 'whose'. The latter is not declined
   and refers to masculine nouns only, e.g.
   Gospódu, čígar híšo vídiš, čésto prodájam
       knjíge. 'I frequently sell books to the
       gentleman whose house you see.'
   If the noun of reference is not masculine,
   the proper case form of the relative pronoun
   katéri would be used in place of čígar:
   Gospodínji, katére híšo vídiš, prodájam
       knjíge. 'I sell books to the lady whose
       house you see.'
   Glédi skózi ôkno, katérega vídiš.
       'Look through the window which you see.'
   [See p. 108 for an explanation on the use of
   the genitive case in the preceding example.]

4. The indeclinable ki is a relative pronoun
   meaning 'who' or 'which'. When appearing in
   the function of the nominative case, ki requires no pronoun. When functioning in any
   other case, ki must be used in combination
   with a short form (clitic) of a personal pronoun whose gender and number agrees with the
   noun of the main clause to which it refers.
   The case of the pronoun, however, is governed
   by the verb or preposition of the relative
   clause, e.g.
       knjíga, ki je bilà na mízi
           'the book which was on the table'
       to je tísti fànt, ki takó lepó pôje
           'that's the same boy who sings so
           beautifully'
                   BUT
       člôvek, ki ga vídiš
           'the person whom you see'
       pšeníca, ki jo kupúješ
           'the wheat which you are buying'
       ljudjé, ki jim govoríš
           'the people to whom you are speaking'

očí, ki v njìh igrá vesêlje
   'the eyes in which joy plays'
znánec, ki ga ne oménjaš pogósto
   'an acquaintance whom you don't
   mention frequently'

5. The unstressed particle le is frequently used
   with pronouns (as with adverbs - see p. 44)
   in Slovene and serves to emphasize a word or
   phrase. When it precedes the word, it is
   joined by a dash, and when it follows it is
   written together with the word, e.g.

   Vprašáli smo tístole žêno
                  or
   Vprašáli smo le-tó žêno.
       'We asked that very woman.'
   In the second example a form of le-tá occurs.
   It may also be written as tále. Pronouns which
   can be combined with le include ônale / le-ôna
   'she!', tákšnale 'such a one!' and others.

NUMERALS

The two main categories of numerals in Slovene are: **cardinal** and **ordinal**. A list of them follows:

	cardinal		ordinal
0	nìč [núla]		[níčti/núlti]
1	èn (êden), êno, êna		pŕvi
2	dvá, dvé		drúgi
3	tríje, trí		trétji
4	štírje, štíri		četŕti
5	pét		pêti
6	šést		šêsti
7	sédem		sêdmi
8	ósem		ôsmi
9	devét		devêti
10	desét		desêti
11	enájst		enájsti
12	dvánajst		dvanájsti
13	trínajst		trinájsti
14	štírinajst		štirinájsti
15	pétnajst		petnájsti
16	šéstnajst		šestnájsti
17	sédemnajst		sedemnájsti
18	ósemnajst		osemnájsti
19	devétnajst		devetnájsti
20	dvájset		dvájseti
21	ênaindvájset	[note!]	ênaindvájseti
22	dváindvájset	[note!]	dváindvájseti
23	tríindvájset	[note!]	tríindvájseti
24	štíriindvájset	[note!]	štíriindvájseti
25	pétindvájset	[note!]	pétindvájseti
30	trídeset		trídeseti
40	štírideset		štírideseti
50	pétdeset		pétdeseti
60	šéstdeset		šéstdeseti
70	sédemdeset		sédemdeseti
80	ósemdeset		ósemdeseti
90	devétdeset		devétdeseti
100	stó		stôti
101	stó êna		stó pŕvi
200	dvésto		dvéstoti
300	trísto		trístoti
400	štíristo		štíristoti

500	pétsto	pétstoti
600	šéststo	šéststoti
700	sédemsto	sédemstoti
800	ósemsto	ósemstoti
900	devétsto	devétstoti
1000	tísoč	tísoči
1001	tísoč êna	tísoč pŕvi
2000	dvá tísoč	dvátísoči
3000	trí tísoč	trítísoči
4000	štíri tísoč	štíritísoči
5000	pét tísoć	péttísoči
100,000	stó tísoč	stótísoči
1,000,000	milijón	milijónski/milijónti
2,000,000	dvá milijóna	dvamilijónti
3,000,000	tríje milijóni	trimilijónti
4,000,000	štírje milijóni	štirimilijónti
5,000,000	pét milijónov	petmilijónti
1,000,000,000	milijárda	milijárden

Some fractions have their own special forms, e.g.

1/2	êna polovíca
1/3	êna tretjína
1/4	êna četrtína OR èn četŕt
1/5, 1/6	êna petína, êna šestína, etc.

In comparing cardinal and ordinal numerals, the student will note that ordinals from 'fifth' onward are formed by the addition of the suffix -i to the cardinal, e.g. pét + i = pêti. The cardinals sédem and ósem drop the final -e [ə]. The cardinal stó and its compounds take the suffix -ti, as does milijón (which also has an alternate form in -ski), as well as the rarely used níčti/núlti. Milijárden adds the suffix -en [ən]. The ordinals pŕvi, drúgi, trétji and četŕti should be learned as separate vocabulary items. [Observe accent and stress changes from cardinal to ordinal!]

In the preceding list the numerals from 100,000 to 1,000,000,000 are given in their American style, i.e. with commas. The learner is reminded that Slovene, in standard European style, uses the comma to set off millions (1,000,000 = 1,000.000) and to designate fractions ('three tenths' = 0,3). Further, in printed texts when numerals are followed by no punctuation they are to be read as cardinals. A period (i.e. decimal point) is used to indicate ordinals and to set off thousands:

    1, 8, 3   = êna ('one' is read as feminine),
                   ósem, trí
    1., 8., 3.   = pŕvi, ôsmi, trétji
    100.000   = stó tísoč

DECLENSIONS

        The cardinal numeral 'one' occurs in the singular and is declined like bogàt (p. 33). The cardinals 'two', 'three' and 'four' share a substantial number of endings in common with dual and plural endings for adjectives but display a number of endings which require special attention. Each of the preceding is presented in its entirity below. Ordinal numerals are adjectives, e.g. pŕvi, pŕva, pŕva 'first' and are declined like bogáti (see p. 37 and note 2.(c) on p. 38).

	(m)	(n)	(f)
N	êden / èn	êno	êna
A	N/G	N	êno
G		ênega	êne
D		ênemu	êni
L		ênem	êni
I		ênim	êno

The numerals 'two', 'three' and 'four' distinguish gender in the nominative and accusative cases:

	(m)			(n/f)		
N	dvá	tríje	štírje	dvé	trí	štíri
A	dvá	trí	štíri	dvé	trí	štíri
G		dvéh	tréh	štírih		
D		dvéma	trém	štírim		
L		dvéh	tréh	štírih		
I		dvéma	trémi	štírimi		

Numerals from 5 to 99 do not distinguish gender and are declined like adjectives in the genitive,

dative, locative and instrumental plural. 'Five'
is declined below.

N/A	pét
G	pêtih
D	pêtim
L	pêtih
I	pêtimi

Case agreement with numerals

(a) The number 'one' is an adjective and modifies
nouns in the singular. If a verb appears in the
sentence, it is also in the singular. The special
masculine form êden stands alone, i.e. does not
act as a modifier:

> Imá pét otrôk, pa je le êden njêmu
> podóben.
> 'He has five children, but only one
> resembles him.'
> En sám gospód je príšel.
> 'Just one gentleman arrived.'

(b) The number 'two' is a dual, and the noun
and verb occurring with it are also in the dual:

> Dvá gospóda sta prišlà.
> 'Two gentlemen arrived.'

(c) The numbers 'three' and 'four' behave like
plural adjectives, as do the nouns which they
modify. The verb is also in the plural:

> Tríje/štírje gospódje so prišlì.
> 'Three/four gentlemen arrived.'

(d) When used in the nominative case, the numbers 'five' and higher require that nouns and
adjectives which follow be in the genitive
plural. In all other cases the numbers, nouns
and adjectives agree in case. The verb, however,
occurs in the third person neuter singular:

> Pét gospódov je prišló.
> 'Five gentlemen arrived.'
> Desét lépih deklét se je pogovárjalo.
> 'Ten pretty girls were talking.'

NOTES ON NUMERALS

1. **Stó** 'one hundred' is declined like **pét**: **stó,
   stôtih**, etc. (A special form **stótina** exists
   to indicate groups of one hundred and is used
   in both the singular and plural, e.g. **stótine
   ljudí** 'hundreds of people'). The numeral **tísoč**
   'one thousand' is declined like a masculine noun

2. In practical terms there is a tendency not to
   decline numerals other than digits and simple
   multiples of tens in the spoken language. At
   the early stages of language learning, the
   student of Slovene will need to know certain
   forms of numeral declensions, e.g. those which
   will be needed in telling time: **ob šêstih** 'at
   six o'clock' (see pp. 114-115).

3. By the addition of the suffix **-krat** to cardinal
   numbers, one obtains an adverb of frequency:
   ênkrat 'once', **dvákrat** 'twice', etc. Examples:
   > **ênkrat na dán**
   >> 'once a day'
   > **Bíl je ênkrat tóčen.**
   >> 'He was punctual for once.'
   > **Òn je dvákrat staréjši od mêne.**
   >> 'He's twice as old as I.'
   > **Dánes sem ga dvákrat vídel.**
   >> 'I saw him twice today.'

4. By adding the suffix **-ič** to ordinal numerals, one obtains an adverb of time:
   > **pŕvič** 'firstly', 'for the first time'
   > **drúgič** 'secondly', 'for the second time'

   Examples:
   > **Pŕvič sem v Ljubljáni.**
   >> 'This is my first time in Ljubljana.'
   > **drúgič se oženíti**
   >> 'to get married for the second time'
   > **Včásih se šáli, drúgič kričí.**
   >> 'Sometimes he jokes, and at other
   >> times he shouts.'

5. The word **obá / obé** 'both' behaves in all
   respects like **dvá / dvé**, including in its

declension (obéh, obéma). Compare the case
forms with the declensions of tá and vès.
[Note: Native speakers feel dvá / dvé and
obá / obé to be pronouns.]

6. Slovene has collective numerals, i.e. words
used to indicate groups or units. They are
declined like adjectives.

(a) There are the special forms enój, dvój,
trój and četvér. Higher collectives are
formed by adding the stressed suffix -ér to
the cardinal form of the numeral, e.g. petér,
tisočér. They are used with nouns which have
no singular, e.g. dvója vráta 'two doors' or
to designate the number of different types of
an object, e.g. sedméra vína 'seven varieties
of wine'.

(b) The neuter singular form may be used to
designate groups of people or objects. In
such cases the noun follows in the genitive
plural, e.g. desetéro ljudí 'a group of ten
persons'.

[See also note. 1. above concerning stótina.]

PREPOSITIONS

Each preposition in Slovene requires the use of one or more cases when used with nouns and adjectives. In those instances where the same preposition may be used with more than one case, its meaning changes. Compare, for instance, the preposition z (s) when it requires the genitive case and when used with the instrumental case. A list of the most common prepositions and the cases which they govern follows accompanied by illustrative phrases. The translations attempt to provide each preposition's basic meaning, but the learner is reminded that some prepositions, e.g. za 'for', cover a wider variety of senses than can be expressed by a single "equivalent" in English. The examples each indicate one possible meaning of the given preposition.

GENITIVE

blízu   'near'
Vóz je blízu híše.
'The car is near the house.'

brez   'without'
híša brez vŕta
'a house without a garden'

do   'up to' / 'till'
do danášnjega dné
'up to this day'

iz   'from' / 'out of'
príti iz Ljubljáne
'to come from Ljubljana'

ízmed   'from among'
Ízmed híš se je slíšal krík.
'A cry was heard from among the houses.'

íznad   '(from) above'
Òn je visôko íznad njìh.
'He towers high above them.'

ízpod   'from under'
Vôda têče ízpod skále.
'Water flows from under the cliff.'

ízpred   'from in front of'
Odpeljál je ízpred híše.

60

'He left from in front of the house.'

ízza 'from behind'
Sónce síje ízza obláka.
'The sun shines from behind the cloud.'

mímo 'by' / 'past'
Šlà je mímo cérkve.
'She walked past the church.'

namésto 'instead of'
Pójdi tjà namesto mêne.
'Go there in my stead.'

od '(away) from'
pót od Ljubljáne do Zágreba
'the way from Ljubljana to Zagreb'

okóli / okróg 'around'
Pogóvor se je súkal okóli polítike.
'The conversation revolved around
                                politics.'

okróg pêtih
'around five o'clock'

póleg 'beside'
hodíti póleg njé
'to walk beside her'

préko 'across'
préko hríbov in dolín
'the length and breadth of the country'
   (= 'across the hills and valleys')

rázen 'except'
vsì rázen mêne
'everybody except me'

srédi 'in the middle of'
srédi oceána
'in the middle of the ocean'

z (s) 'off of' / 'from'
z míze vzéti
'to take (something) off of the table'
s téga stalíšča
'from that point of view'
   [See end notes for spelling of z / s.]

zarádi 'because of'
Zarádi bolézni je ostàl domá.
'He stayed home because of illness.'

zráven 'beside'
Šóla je zráven cérkve.
'The school is next to (beside) the
                                church.'

DATIVE

k   'to' / 'towards'
           Grém k odvétniku.
           'I'm going to (my) lawyer's.'
           h glávi
           '(pointed) towards the head'
      [See end notes for spelling of k as h.]
kljub   'in spite of'
           Kljub tému vsèmu ní sréčen.
           'In spite of all that he's not happy.'
próti   'towards'
           próti začétku léta
           'towards the beginning of summer'

ACCUSATIVE

čez   'across'
           íti čez réko
           'to go across the river'
med   'among'
           pásti med rázbojnike
           'to fall among thieves'
na   'onto' / 'at'
           Okno gléda na úlico.
           'The window looks onto the street.'
           na prvi poglèd
           'at first sight'
nad   '(to go) above'
           Mèč mu je vísel nad glávo.
           'The sword hung above his head.'
ob   'against'
           ob mízo udáriti
           'to bang against the table'
po   '(to go) for' / 'to get'
           posláti po zdrávnika
           'to send for a doctor'
pod   '(to go) under'
           Dájte tó pod kljúč.
           'Put it under lock and key.'
pred   '(to go) in front of'
           Prédme naj ne hôdi. [see note on p. 49]
           'Don't walk in front of me.'

skóz(i) 'through'
    poglédati skóz(i) ôkno
    'to look out (through) the window'
v   'into'
    Grém v híšo.
    'I'm going into the house.'
za   for' / '(to go) behind'
    vstópnica za gledalíšče
    'a ticket for the theater'
    Sónce gré za gôro.
    'The sun is going behind the mountain.'
zóper   'against'
    Sem zóper tó.
    'I'm against that.'

LOCATIVE

na   'on'
    Víno je na mízi.
    'The wine is on the table.'
o   'about'
    govoríti o vôjni
    'to talk about war'
ob   'at' (in time expressions) / 'by'
    ob tréh [see p. 91]
    'at three o'clock'
    drevó ob Sávi
    'a tree by the Sava (river)'
po   'after'
    po božíču
    'after Christmas'
pri   'at' / 'near'
    pri vášem brátu
    'at your brother's (place)'
    pri ôknu
    'near the window'
v   'in'
    bíti v Ljubljáni
    'to be in Ljubljana'

INSTRUMENTAL

med   'between'
    med nébom in zemljó
    'between heaven and earth'

nad   'above'
             Sónce je nad obzórjem.
             'The sun is above the horizon.'
pod   'under'
             sedéti pod drevésom
             'to sit under the tree'
pred   'in front of'
             Vóz je pred híšo.
             'The car is in front of the house.'
z (s)   'with'
             z vsò močjó
             'with all one's might'
             vstáti s sóncem
             'to get up with the sun'
   [See end notes for spelling of z/s.]
za   'behind' / 'after'
             Za híšo je vŕt.
             'There's a garden behind the house.'
             êden za drúgim
             'one after another'

NOTES TO PREPOSITIONS

1. The preposition z/s is used with the genitive
   and instrumental cases. It is spelled z when
   used before a word beginning with a voiced
   consonant or with a vowel. Likewise, s is
   used before a word beginning with a voiceless
   consonant (see pp. 19-20), e.g.
             z ávtom   'by car'
             z dédom   'with grandfather'
                     but
             s póšto   'by mail'
             s tebój   'with you'

2. The preposition k is used with the dative
   case. It is spelled h when it comes before
   a k or g, e.g.
             h kônju '[to walk] towards the horse'
             h glávi '[to point] towards the head'

VERBS

Slovene has a rich verbal system. There are special **forms** for the **infinitive** and **supine**, described below, as well as sets of forms which change by person (**conjugation**). The verb in Slovene is further characterized by the category of **tense** (**present, past** and **future**) and by **mood** (**indicative, imperative, optative, conditional**), **aspect** (**imperfective** and **perfective**) and **voice** (**active, passive** and **medium**). Finally, it has **participles** (adjectival and adverbial) which are derived from verbs and also have sets of forms. Each of the preceding is summarized below with a more detailed treatment of each provided throughout this chapter.

INFINITIVE

Slovene verbs are entered in the dictionary in their infinitive form. The vast majority of verbs have an infinitive ending in -ti, with a small number ending in -či.(The -i is not normally pronounced in conversational Slovene in the Ljubljana area.)

Examples:

délati	*'to work'*
mísliti	*'to think'*
sésti	*'to sit down'*
kupováti	*'to buy'*
pisáti	*'to write'*
dvígniti	*'to lift'*
razuméti	*'to understand'*
nêsti	*'to carry'*
rêči	*'to say'*
molčáti	*'to be silent'*
vídeti	*'to see'*
čúti	*'to hear'*
píti	*'to drink'*
príti	*'to arrive'*

SUPINE

As opposed to the infinitive ending in -ti or -či, the supine has the endings -t or -č.

It is used after verbs of motion such as *íti* 'to go', **príti** 'to arrive', **hodíti** 'to walk', **peljá-ti** 'to lead' and **tềči** 'to run', seen in the following examples:

infinitive	supine
délati	*Grém délat.*
	'I'm going to work.'
lé̀či	*Pójdi lé̀č.*
	'go lie down!'
nakupováti	*Šlà̀ je nakupovàt.*
	'She went shopping.'
pềči	*Grém pềč.*
	'I'm going to bake.'
pisáti	*Têci písat.*
	'Run off to write.'

It should be noted that supine forms do not necessarily coincide with the shortened conversational forms of the infinitive. In some cases there is a different accent:

infinitive long/short forms	supine
délati / délat	*délat*
but	
lé̀či / lè̀č	*lé̀č*
spáti / spàt	*spát*

PERSON AND CONJUGATION

The present tense is conjugated with a set of endings for three persons in all three numbers: singular, dual and plural. The present tense of the Slovene verb is divided into four basic classes in this presentation, with a fifth residual group of verbs which have irregular conjugations.

TENSE

There are three tenses in Slovene: the **present, past** and **future.** The present tense is simple, i.e. it is non-compound, while the past

and future tenses are compound and are formed by
combining conjugated forms of the verb **bíti** 'to
be' with the participle in -l, normally called
the **descriptive participle**. In older literature
one may encounter the compound **past perfect**
tense, no longer in active use and not presented
here.

MOOD

Mood indicates the speaker's attitude
about an action or condition. This may be expressed in four ways in Slovene:
1.) The **indicative** mood is used to express
   factual statements or elicit information
   as in the following question and reply
   (statement):
   Kám gréš?   **Grém domóv.**
   'Where are you going?' 'I'm going home.'
2.) The **imperative** mood is used in order to
   express commands and requests. It has
   sets of forms for the second person singular and the first and second persons
   of the dual and plural.
3.) The **optative** mood is used as an indirect
   appeal for the involvement of a person in
   an action. It does not have a separate
   set of endings but rather requires the
   use of a special particle coupled with
   the regular verbal forms of the first
   person singular and the third persons
   singular, dual and plural.
4.) The **conditional** mood in Slovene is used
   to express potential events. It is formed
   with the particle **bi** in combination with
   the descripive participle in -l.

ASPECT

Verbs in Slovene are classified by **aspect**.
Most are either **imperfective** or **perfective**, with
a small number being considered biaspectual. The
imperfective aspect denotes actions in progress
or actions which are without limit or which are
repeated. The perfective aspect denotes a momentary or limited action, i.e. one with a specific

completed result. Additionally, verbs in Slovene form aspectual pairs, the imperfective and perfective partners of which are derived in a number of ways discussed later in this chapter.

VOICE

Voice indicates the relationship between the subject and the action expressed by a the verb. Slovene grammarians traditionally recognize three categories of voice: **active, passive** (which is limited to past passive participles) and **medium** (middle).

The active and passive voices subsume the categories of **transitive** and **intransitive**. A transitive verb is one which is capable of expressing an action carried from the subject to the object as in the following sentences:

Véra píše písmo.
'Vera is writing a letter.'
Bêrem knjígo.
'I'm reading a book.'

An intransitive verb cannot take a direct object as in the following sentences:

Véra spí.
'Vera is sleeping.'
Híša je goréla dvá dní.
'The house burned for two days.'

Medium (middle) voice refers to actions which return to the person engaging in them. The category includes for the most part reflexive verbs which are discussed later in this chapter in greater detail, e.g.

Máma se umíva.
'Mother washes herself.'

PARTICIPLES

Slovene has five participles:
1.) Slovene has two **adverbial participles**. They are derived from verbs and are used to describe actions concurrent with the action of the verb of the main clause or which precede that action in time.

2.) **Adjectival participles** are of two kinds: The first type includes the **present** and **past** (**passive**) participles. They behave as adjectives, i.e. they can modify nouns and are fully declined like other adjectives. The former is an active one, and the latter is a passive one. The **descriptive participle in -l** is the second type of adjectival participle. It is used in forming the non-present tenses (past and future) and the conditional mood and denotes gender and number only.

ORGANIZATION AND CLASSIFICATION OF VERBS

The morphology of the verb in Slovene has been described by grammarians and linguists in a number of different ways. The approach used here is one which distinguishes infinitive and present tense stems. The infinitive and present tense stems coincide in many verbs, but often they do not. Establishing a basic division between the two stems will help the student to better understand the structure of the Slovene verb, organized on the formal oppostion of the infinitive and present tense stems, and to create its various sets of forms.

A Slovene verb will be encountered in a given **form** which could be the infinitive (the dictionary entry) form, a present tense form, the imperative, or other. For each new verb it is recommended that the student learn the following forms: the **infinitive** from whose stem one can automatically generate the supine and the past participles, including the descriptive participle in -l; the first person singular **and** third person plural of the **present tense**, from one or both of which the imperative and present participles can be generated. Further, it is helpful to understand that verbs consist of several elements, the most basic of which is its **root.** For example, the root of the infinitive 'to walk'/'to go on foot' **hodíti** is **hod-**. (See also p. 131 for nouns derived from this same root.) The root carries a basic meaning, which can be modified by the addition of a **prefix** as in **obhodíti** 'to make one's rounds'. (See p. 91 for a list of verbal prefixes.)

Suffixes may be added after the verbal root. They do not change the basic meaning of the verb. They create a **stem** which serves as the base onto which **endings** will be added. For example, in the case of **hodíti** the infinitive suffix -i- is added to the root **hod-** creating the stem to which the infinitive ending is added: **hod-** + **-i-** + **-ti** = **hodíti**. Infinitive suffixes are the following: -#-, -a-, -ova-, -i--, -e- and -ni-. (Compare this list to the infinitives presented on p. 65.) Present tense suffixes are the following: -#-, -a-, -i, -e- and -uj-. Reconciling the infinitive and present tense stems is explained in the notes on the present tense conjugation.

Endings may be single, i.e. the infinitive ending, or may come in sets, i.e. those for the various tenses. They are either **personal** or **non-personal**. Personal endings, i.e. endings which change according to the subject of the verb, are those which appear in the sections below treating the conjugation of the tense forms and the formation of the imperative. All other endings for Slovene verbs are non-personal and include the infinitive, the supine and all participles. (Adjectival participles indicate gender, but **not** person.)

CONJUGATION OF THE PRESENT TENSE

With the exception of the third person plural, there is a one set of endings for the conjugation of the present tense. The selection of the correct ending of the third person plural is seen on the following chart and is described in the notes. The present tense conjugations are divided into four basic classes. A fifth class includes a number of irregular verbs, and these are treated separately on pp. 89-91. When comparing the four conjugations which follow with the list of infinitives given on p. 67, one may note that the list includes verbs with the

following infinitive suffixes attached to their
roots:

    -a-   (délati, pisáti and molčáti)
    -i-   (mísliti)
    -e-   (vídeti and razuméti)
    -ni-   (dvígniti)
    -ova-   (kupováti)
    -#-   (nêsti, sésti, rêči, čúti,
               píti, and príti).

        The number of suffixes to which endings
are added in the present tense is smaller (-#-,
-a-, -i-, -e-, and -uj-). They behave in a pre-
dictable fashion with regard to sets of forms
and endings, explained for each category in the
notes which follow. Further, only one of three
vowels, -a-, -i- and -e-, may precede the endings of the present tense. The verbs razuméti,
mísliti and délati retain those vowels in both
the infinitive and present tense stems, and the
present tense endings are added directly to the
stems. The verbs molčáti and vídeti take the
vowel -i- as their suffix in the present tense
and are conjugated like mísliti. The verb dvígniti takes the suffix -e- as do all remaining
verbs in the list above. They have a -#- suffix
to which the vowel -e- is added before the endings:

    nêsti   ~   nes#- + -e-
    rêči   ~   reč#- + -e- (root = rek-)
    sésti   ~   ses#- < sed#- + -e-
    pisáti ~   pis#- > piš#- + -e-
    príti   ~   prid#- + -e-
    kupováti ~ kupuj#- + -e-
    čúti   ~   čuj#- + -e-
    píti   ~   pij#- + -e-

                Present tense endings

          singular   dual   plural
1.   -m   -va   -mo
2.   -š   -ta   -te
3.   -#   -ta   -jo/-e/-o

```
┌─────────────────────────────────────────┐
│      PRESENT TENSE CONJUGATIONS          │
└─────────────────────────────────────────┘
```

infinitive	délati	mísliti
	'to work'	'to think'
singular		
1.	délam	míslim
2.	délaš	mísliš
3.	déla	mísli
dual		
1.	délava	mísliva
2.- 3.	délata	míslita
plural		
1.	délamo	míslimo
2.	délate	míslite
3.	délajo	míslijo

infinitive	nêsti	kupováti
	'to carry'	'to buy'
singular		
1.	nêsem	kupújem
2.	nêseš	kupúješ
3.	nêse	kupúje
dual		
1.	nêseva	kupújeva
2.- 3.	nêseta	kupújeta
plural		
1.	nêsemo	kupújemo
2.	nêsete	kupújete
3.	nêsejo/nesó	kupújejo

NOTES ON THE PRESENT TENSE CONJUGATION

1. Verbs of the type délati and mísliti are among the most common types of verbs encountered in Slovene. As can be seen above, the vowel, if any, of the infinitive suffix is not a reliable guide for the vowel to which the present tense verbal endings are to be added. That is the reason why the student is encouraged to learn each verb in its infini-

tive form (the form in which it is listed in
dictionaries), the first person singular and
the third person plural. The latter is also
necessary because of the variants often found
here (see footnote 8. below). The chart below
summarizes the infinitive and present tense
suffixes and is followed by notes which will
provide hints on reconciling the choice of
the vowel to be used in the conjugation of
the present tense:

infinitive suffix	vowel of present tense	
-#-	-e-	nêsti, sésti, rêči, čúti, píti, príti
-a-	-a- -i- -e-	délati molčáti pisáti
-ova- (> -uj-)	-e-	kupováti
-i-	-i-	mísliti
-e-	-i- -e-	vídeti razuméti
-ni-	-e-	dvígniti

OR

The chart which follows arranges the same
information in a different way, presenting
the present tense vowels and suffixes:

present tense vowel	present tense suffix	
-a-	-a-	délati
-i-	-i-	mísliti vídeti molčati
all others -e-	-#- -uj-	nêsti, rêči sésti, príti kupováti (includes čúti and píti) razuméti dvígniti pisáti

2. (a) As can be seen, verbs which have an -a-
   in the stem of the infinitive require special
   attention from the learner. The vast majority
   of them retain that -a- in the present tense
   and are conjugated like délati. It should be
   noted that verbs in this class **always** add a
   -j- to their stem when used to create other
   forms derived from the present stem (e.g. the
   imperative and active participles):
                    dela- > delaj-.

   (b) A number of verbs with an infinitive in
   -ati, always preceded by the soft consonants
   -š-, -ž- or -č-, take the vowel -i- in the
   present tense, e.g.
   'to hear'   slišati ~ slíšim ~ slíšijo
   'to lie'   ležáti ~ ležím ~ ležíjo
   'to be silent' molčáti ~ molčím ~ molčíjo

   The presence of a soft consonant does not
   always mean that the verb behaves as those
   noted above. Some of them are also conjugated
   like délati, e.g.
   'to pay' plačáti ~ pláčam ~ pláčajo
   'to end' končáti ~ končám ~ končájo

(c) A significant group of verbs with an -a-
in the infinitive stem display an alternation
of the root consonant (see consonant alternations on pp. 20-21) in all forms of the present tense. Such verbs take the vowel -e- in
the present tense, e.g.
'to write'   pisáti ~ píšem ~ píšejo
'to seek'   iskáti ~ íščem ~ iščejo

Included here also are the verbs:
'to lead' peljáti ~ péljem ~ péljejo
'to call' klicáti ~ klíčem ~ klíčejo
'to take' jemáti ~ jêmljem ~ jêmljejo

(d) Verbs whose infinitive ends in -ovati (or
-evati) are conjugated like kupováti,i.e. the
-ova-/-eva- suffix of the infinitive contracts
to form a present tense suffix in -uj-, and
the vowel of the present tense is -e-. A very
small number of other verbs which have the
vowel -i- or -u- before the infinitive ending
-ti also have a present tense stem ending in
-j-. They belong to this category as well and
include the verbs:
'to drink'   píti ~ píjem ~ píjejo
'to hear'   čúti ~ čújem ~ čújejo

3. Most verbs which have an -i- in the infinitive stem retain that -i- in the present
   tense and are conjugated like mísliti, e.g.
   'to praise' hvalíti ~ hválim ~ hválijo
   'to speak' govoríti ~ govorím ~ govoríjo
   'to exclude' izkljúčiti ~ izkljúčim ~
                izkljúčijo

   [Note: See 2 (d) above for the conjugation
    of píti.]

4. (a) Verbs with an -e- in the infinitive stem
   take the vowel -i- or -e- in the present tense
   and must be learned individually. The group of
   verbs which take the vowel -i- in the present
   includes:
   'to see' vídeti ~ vídim ~ vídijo
   'to live' živéti ~ živím ~ živíjo

'to burn' **goréti ~ gorím ~ goríjo**
'to sit' **sedéti ~ sedím ~ sedíjo**

(b) To the group of verbs which take the
vowel -e- in the present tense belong the
verbs:
'to understand' **razuméti ~ razúmem ~**
                 razúmejo
'to be allowed' **sméti ~ smém ~ sméjo**

5. In verbs with an infinitive suffix in -ni-
   that suffix is replaced by -ne- in the present tense, e.g.
   'to lift'   **dvígniti ~ dvígnem ~ dvígnejo**
   'to set out' **kreníti ~ krénem ~ krénejo**

6. (a) Verbs with a -#- stem in both the infinitive and present tense such as **nêsti** take the
   vowel -e- as a suffix in the present tense.
   [Note:In the absence of a vowel, the root and
   the stem of the infinitive are the same]. The
   infinitive ending is added directly to the
   final consonant of the root, as is the vowel
   -e- of the present tense.
   (In the case of 'to sit down' **sésti ~ sédem ~**
   sédejo the alternation of **s ~ d** between the
   infinitive and the present tense and participle in -l (**sédel**) is exceptional and is not
   found among the consonant alternations given
   on pp. 20-21. Such information is normally
   provided in dictionaries.)

   (b) All verbs whose infinitives end in -či
   belong here. Their present tense forms have
   either -č- or -ž- throughout their conjugations. The root consonant of those verbs is
   either a -k- or a -g-. Although not apparent
   from the infinitive, the descriptive participle in -l- will reveal the root consonant.
   Alternatively, one may be guided by the fact
   that those with a -č- in the present tense
   have a root in -k-, and those with -ž- have
   a root in -g-, e.g.
        'to lie down' **léči ~ léžem ~ légel**

Some verbs display the -k- or -g- in alternate forms for the third person plural, e.g.
'to say' rêči ~ rêčem ~ rêčejo/rekó ~ rékel.
(See also the following section on past and
future tenses.)

[Note: The verb môči does not follow the
preceding pattern. It has a special conjugation. See p. 90.]

7. There is a mixed group of verbs in common use
   whose stem present tense stem cannot be pre-
   dicted on the basis of information provided
   in the preceding analysis. Their conjugations
   must be learned individually.

   (a) The following verbs take the vowel -e- in
   the present tense:
   'to read'   bráti ~ bêrem ~ bêrejo
   'to select'   izbráti~ izbêrem~ izbêrejo
   'to arrive'   príti ~ prídem ~ prídejo '
   'to begin'   začéti ~ začnèm ~ začnèjo/začnó
   'to take'   vzéti ~ vzámem ~ vzámejo
   'to sing'   péti   ~ pôjem ~ pôjejo

   (b) The following verbs take the vowel -i- in
   the present tense:
   'to fear'   báti se~ bojím se~ bojíjo se
   'to sleep'   spáti ~   spím ~ spíjo
   'to stand'   státi ~   stojím ~ stojíjo

   (c) See pp. 89-90 for the special conjugations of the following verbs:
                 bíti   'to be'
                 jésti   'to eat'
                 dáti   'to give'
                 védeti 'to know'
                 íti   'to go'
                 iméti   'to have'
                 hotéti 'to want'
                 môči   'to be able'.

8. (a) A number of verbs of the type nêsti 'to
   lead' have short alternate forms in the third
   person plural: nêsejo / nesó. Similarly: 'to

begin' začéti ~ začnêjo / začnó. The short
form is always stressed on the final syllable.

(b) Likewise, a few verbs whose ending is
normally a stressed -íjo in the third person
plural (of the mísliti type of conjugation)
may take an alternate ending, also stressed,
in -é. The longer forms are preferred in the
contemporary spoken language, while the short
forms may be found in older literature or in
dialects. Examples:

'to hurry'   hitéti ~ hitíjo / hité
'to lie'   ležáti ~ ležíjo / ležé
'to live'   živéti ~ živíjo / živé

PAST AND FUTURE TENSES

FORMATION OF THE DESCRIPTIVE PARTICIPLE IN -l

The past and future tenses in Slovene
are compound formations consisting of an
auxiliary verb plus the descriptive participle
in -l. That participle is coupled with the
present tense of the verb bíti 'to be' in order
to express a past tense and with the future
tense of the same verb to express the future.
When functioning as an auxiliary, forms of the
verb 'to be' are unstressed. Its conjugations
are presented in the charts which follow and on
p. 89. The participle expresses gender and
number, while the auxiliary verb denotes person
and tense. The descriptive participle in -l is
formed from the infinitive stem by the simple
addition of the -l to the final vowel of the
stem, e.g. 'to speak' govor-+-i-+-ti = govoríti,
likewise govor-+-i-+-l = govoríl, govoríla, etc.
Verbs with an infinitive stem in -#- ending in a
consonant (including all verbs with the infinitive ending -či) add an -e- [ə] before the -l
of the descriptive participle for the masculine
singular form only. The following list provides
the masculine and feminine descriptive participle in -l of the all verbs shown in the
analysis in note 1. on pp. 72-74:

délati ~ délal / délala
pisáti ~ písal / pisála
molčáti ~ mólčal / molčála
kupováti ~ kupovàl / kupovála
mísliti ~ míslil / míslila
dvígniti ~ dvígnil / dvígnila
vídeti ~ vídel / vídela
razuméti ~ razúmel /razuméla
píti ~ píl /píla
čúti ~ čúl / čúla
nêsti ~ nésel / nêsla
sésti ~ sédel / sédla
rêči ~ rékel / rêkla

Note that, in the verb **sésti** the **-l** is added
to the root **-d-** (see note 6.(a) above) with an
-e- [ə] inserted in the masculine form. Likewise, verbs in **-či** have in their root either **-k-**
or **-g-** (the root consonant of each of these
verbs before alternation) which is used to form
the descriptive participle as seen in **rêči** and
léči. (see note in 6.(b) above)

PAST TENSE

'to work'		masculine	feminine	neuter
singular				
1.	sem	délal	délala	délalo
2.	si	"	"	"
3.	je	"	"	"
dual				
1.	sva	délala	délali	délali
2. - 3.	sta	"	"	"
plural				
1.	smo	délali	délale	délala
2.	ste	"	"	"
3.	so	"	"	"

FUTURE TENSE

'to speak'	masculine	feminine	neuter
singular			
1. bom	govóril	govoríla	govorílo
2. boš	"	"	"
3. bo	"	"	"
dual			
1. bova	govoríla	govoríli	govoríli
2. - 3. bosta	"	"	"
plural			
1. bomo	govoríli	govoríle	govoríla
2. boste	"	"	"
3. bodo	"	"	"

IMPERATIVE

       Comands and strong requests in Slovene may be issued in the second person singular, dual and plural, as well as in the first person dual and plural. The **basic form of the imperative** is that of the second person singular. It is formed from the present tense stem. There are two possible suffixes, -j- or -i-, to which the following endings are added, as seen below in the verbs **délati** 'to work' and **nêsti** 'to carry':

#, -va, -ta, -mo, -te

singular
-#   2.   délaj   nêsi
           '(you) work / carry!'
dual
-va   1.   délajva   nesíva
         'let's you and I work / carry!'
-ta   2.   délajta   nesíta
         'you two work / carry!'
plural
-mo   1.   délajmo   nesímo
         'let's work / carry!'
-te   2.   délajte   nesíte
         '(you) work / carry!'

Those verbs with a present tense stem in -a- (délati) retain that -a- and add the suffix -j- to the stem (refer to note 2 (a) on p. 74), e.g. délaj-. This creates a stem for the imperative to which the other endings are added in the first and second persons dual plural. Note that the stem of délaj is now equal to that of the verbs kupováti ~ kupúj- (p. 74), čúti ~ čúj, and píti ~ pij- (note 2 (d), p. 75). The vowel -i- is used as a suffix to create the stem, i.e. the basic form, of the imperative for all other verbs, i.e. those with present tense suffixes in -#- or -i- (i.e. those verbs which take the vowels -i- or -e- in the present tense conjugation). This includes all verbs of the type mísliti, vídeti and molčáti, as well as verbs of the type nêsti, sésti, rêči, príti, dvígniti, razuméti and pisáti (See notes 2.-7. on pp. 74-77.). The vowel -i- is added directly to the final consonant of present tense stem. [Note: Verbs with an infinitive in -či have a special alternation of the root consonant: -g->-z- and -k->-c-.]

samples of imperatives

	infinitive / 1st sing.	imperative
'to read'	čítati / čítam	čítaj
'to work'	délati / délam	délaj

and

	infinitive / 1st sing.	imperative
'to buy'	kupováti / kupújem	kupúj
'to hear'	čúti / čújem	čúj
'to drink'	píti / píjem	píj
'to sing'	péti / pôjem	pój

but

	infinitive / 1st sing.	imperative
'to lift'	dvígniti / dvígnem	dvígni
'to speak'	govoríti / govorím	govôri
'to lie down'	léči / léžem	lézi[note!]
'to be silent'	molčáti / molčím	mólči
'to carry'	nêsti / nêsem	nêsi
'to write'	pisáti / píšem	píši
'to arrive'	príti / prídem	prídi
'to understand'	razuméti / razúmem	razúmi

'to say'	rêči / rêčem	rêci[note!]
'to sit'	sedéti / sedím	sêdi
'to sit down'	sésti / sédem	sédi
'to begin'	začéti / začnèm	začnì

OPTATIVE

Slovene has a category of mood, comple-
menting the imperative, called the optative
which exhorts the listener(s) or expresses the
desirability of an event which may be rendered
in English by words such as 'let, 'should' and
'may'. The optative pattern uses existing sets
of verbal forms, namely the present tense in the
first person singular and in the third person
singular, dual and plural before which the particle **naj** is placed:

singular
1. naj délam   'let me work'/'I should work'
3. naj déla   'let him/her/it work'
dual and plural
3. naj délata 'let the two of them work'
3. naj délajo 'let them work'

examples
Naj ti póšljem prepís?
   'Should I send you a copy?'
Vêlel je, naj gredó.
   'He ordered them to go.'
Naj bó!
   'Let it be!'
Naj počíva v míru!
   'May he rest in peace!'
Káj naj storím?
   'What should I do?'
Rêci mu, naj príde!
   'Tell him that he should come!'
Naj stáne, kár hóče!
   'Let is cost what it may!'
Naj ljudí rêčejo, kár hóčejo!
   'Let people say what they will!'
Nísem védel, ali naj se sméjem ali jóčem.
   'I didn't know whether to laugh or cry!'

CONDITIONAL

There are two conditional patterns in Slovene. They are formed using the descriptive participle in -l and the simple addition of the particle **bi**. In compound sentences both the main and the subordinate clauses require that the verb appear in the conditional form.

PRESENT CONDITIONAL: The particle **bi** is accompanied by the descriptive participle in -l. (See p. 78 for its formation.)

Bi mi lahkó pomagáli?
  'Would you (please) help me?'
Bi mi dáli ógenj?
  'Would you give me a light?'
Ne da bi jàz védel.
  'Not as far as I (would) know.'
Jàz bi šèl, ko bi utégnil.
  'I would go if I had time.'
Če bi védel, bi ti povédal.
  'If I knew, I would tell you.'
Ko bi míslil na nevárnost, bi voják v bítki
  znôrel.
  'If he thought about the danger, a
    soldier would become insane in battle.'
Jàz bi délal, če bi me kdo pláčal.
  'I would work if someone would pay me.'
Ona bi šlà na Brézje, če bi jo tí zapêljal
  z ávtom.
  'She would go to Brezje if you would drive
    her.'
Mí ne bi dvígnili cén, če bi ne bilì
  proizvódni stróški takó visôki.
  'We wouldn't raise prices if production
    costs weren't so high.'

PAST CONDITIONAL: The participle **bi** is accompanied by the descriptive participle in -l of the verb 'to be' (**bi bil**) plus the descriptive participle in -l of the action under question. The following sentences illustrate the past conditional, but the learner is cautioned that they are stilted and belong to the literary language.

In conversational Slovene the present conditional would more likely be used:

Če ne bi bil zamúdil tístega letála, bi se
bíl z drúgimi pótniki vréd smŕtno
ponesréčil.
  'If he had not missed that plane, he
  would have been killed with the other
  passengers.'
Ko bi védel, kakó môčna je slívovka, bi je ne
bil spíl cél kozárec na dúšek in se ne bi
bil takó osméšil.
  'If I had known how strong the plum brandy
  was, I would not have drunk a whole glass
  in one gulp and made such an ass of my-
  self.'

PARTICIPLES

As seen above, Slovene has a descriptive participle in -l used to form compound tenses (past and future) and the conditional mood. Beyond that there are two adverbial and two adjectival participles. All five are part of both the written language and of the educated style of spoken Slovene. The two adjectival participles, the present (active) and the (past) passive, behave in all respects like adjectives, i.e. they agree in gender, case and number with the modified noun. In the spoken language adjectival participles are frequently used as simple adjectives, e.g.

Mój bràt je molčéč člôvek.
  'My brother is a reticent (quiet)
  person.' [literally 'remaining silent']
Rečêno, storjêno.
  '(No sooner) said (than) done.'
Césta je zapŕta.
  'The road is closed.'

The two adverbial participles behave as other adverbs in Slovene, with the present adverbial participle describing simultaneous actions, and the past adverbial participle describing antece-

dent actions. Basic rules for the formation of
adjectival and adverbial participles are provided below.

ADVERBIAL PARTICIPLES: Slovene has two adverbial
participles, one with the ending -e/-je and the
other with the ending -vši/-ši. They modify the
main verb of the given sentence.

   The participle in -e/-je denotes an action
simultaneous with the main verb of the sentence.
It is formed from **imperfective** verbs by adding
the vowel -e to the final consonant of the present tense stem (stems in -#-, -i- and -e-). As
was the case in the formation of the imperative,
verbs with a present tense stem in -a- (**délati**)
add an -j- to their stem (p. 80) to which the
ending -e is added.
   (See below for stems in -uj-.)

examples

molčáti ~ molčím ~ molčé 'being silent'
   Molčé so šlì v smŕt.
      'They went to their death silently.'
igráti ~ igrám ~ igráje   'playing'
   Tó bom igráje narédil v pól úre.
      'I'll complete that in half an hour
      (playing)' [= 'It's child's play!]
sésti ~ sédem ~ sedé 'sitting'
   Tó délo lahkó oprávljaš sedé.
   'You can do that while sitting.'

Other examples include:

stojé from **státi** ~ **stojím** 'to stand'
gredé from **íti**   ~ **grém** 'to go'
ležé from **ležáti** ~ **ležím** 'to lie'
kupováje (**kupúje** in an older literary form)
      from **kupováti** ~ **kupújem** 'to buy'
[Note: In the last example there is a tendency
to derive the participle for this class of
verbs from the infinitive stem -ova- by the
addition of -j- + -e rather than from the present
tense stem -uj- so that their formation is like
that for **délati**.]

The participle in -vši/-ši denotes an antecedent action, i.e. one completed before the action of the main verb of the sentence and is derived from **perfective** verbs. It is limited in use primarily to the literary language. It is formed from the infinitive stem to which the ending -vši is added. In the case of verbs without a vowel in the infinitive stem, i.e. those with a -#- stem (including those verbs whose infinitive is -či), the ending -ši is added directly to the root/stem consonant:

> *pozabíti ~ pozábil ~ pozabívši*
> > 'having forgotten'
> *dvígniti ~ dvígnil ~ dvígnivši*
> > 'having raised'
> > **but**
> *rêči ~ rékel ~ rékši* 'having said'
> *sésti ~ sédel ~ sédši* 'having sat down'

> **examples**
> *Sédši k mízi, so začéli jésti.*
> > 'Having sat down at the table, they began to eat.'
> *Pozabívši, da ní domá, je začéla preuréjati sóbo.*
> > 'Forgetting [=Having forgotten] that she wasn't home, she began changing around the room.'
> *«Zdrávo» je rêkla Mílica, vstopívši v híšo.*
> > '"Hello," said Milica, entering [=having entered] the house.'

ADJECTIVAL PARTICIPLES: There are two adjectival participles in Slovene, a present (active) one formed from **imperfective** verbs and a past (passive) one formed from **perfective** verbs. Both behave like adjectives and can be fully declined. The rules for forming adjectival participles are somewhat complex, and there are a number of exceptions.

The **present participle** is formed from the present tense stem. Its ending is -č which is added to the vowel -o- or -e-, the selection of which is described below:

1. (a) Verbs with present tense stems in -uj-
   and -a- (verbs of the type **délati** which
   added -j- in the imperative and adverbial
   participle in -e/-je, do so here again)
   take the ending -óč. [**Note:** It will help
   to compare these forms to the third person
   plural.]
   délati ~ délajo ~ delajóč   'working'
   čákati ~ čákajo ~ čakajóč   'waiting'
   kupováti ~ kupújejo ~ kupujóč   'buying'
   potováti ~ potújejo ~ potujóč   'travelling'

   (b) Verbs which have a present tense stem
   in -#- or -e-, i.e. those which use the
   vowel -e- in the present tense, have a
   third person plural ending in -ejo or -ó.
   They also take the ending -óč, adding it
   to the final consonant of the stem.
   pisáti ~ píšejo ~ pišóč   'writing'
   nêsti ~ nêsejo/nesó ~ nesóč   'carrying'
   bráti ~ bêrejo/beró ~ beróč   'reading'
   rêči   ~ rêčejo/rekó ~ rekóč   'saying'

2. Verbs with a present tense stem in -i- keep
   that vowel throughout the present tense and
   have a third person plural ending in -ijo
   or -é. They take the ending -éč, adding it
   to the final consonant of the stem.
   mísliti ~ míslijo ~ misléč
      'thinking'
   čutíti ~ čútijo ~ čutéč
      'feeling'
   molčáti ~ molčíjo/molčé ~ molčéč
      'being silent'
   ležáti ~ ležíjo/ležé   ~ ležéč
      'lying'
   sedéti ~ sedíjo ~ sedéč
      'sitting'

   The past passive participle is formed
from the infinitive stem of transitive verbs, to
which an -n or -t is added. The vast majority of
verbs with past passive participles belong to
the perfective aspect,but a number in common use
are imperfective (e.g. **kúhan** and **pečèn** below).

1. Verbs which have an infinitive stem in -a-
   or -ova- add -n directly to the -a- of the
   stem, e.g.

napisáti	~ napísan	'written'
kúhati	~ kúhan	'cooked'
kupováti	~ kupován	'purchased'
poškódováti	~ poškódován	'damaged'
pláčáti	~ pláčan	'paid'
razprodáti	~ razprodán	'sold out'
zdélati	~ zdélan	'tired'/'worn out'

2. (a) Those verbs with an infinitive stem in
   -i- take the ending -en added to the final
   consonant of the stem. If that consonant
   is one which can alternate as described on
   pp. 20-21, then that alternation will occur
   before the -en is added.

hvalíti	~ hváljen	'praised'
naváditi(se)	~ navájen	'accustomed to'
oženíti	~ ožénjen	'married'
ponosíti	~ ponóšen	'worn out'
popráviti	~ poprávljen	'fixed'
rániti	~ ránjen	'wounded'
rodíti	~ rôjen	'born'
ulovíti	~ ulovljèn	'caught'
uredíti	~ urejèn	'arranged'
uvozíti	~ uvóžen	'imported'
zapustíti	~ zapuščen	'abandonded'

   [**Note**:   The soft consonants -č-, -ž- and -š-
   are the result of earlier alternations and
   cannot alternate further. Verbs with such
   consonants are included in this group:
   izkljúčiti ~ izkljúčen 'excluded']

   (b) Verbs which have an infinitive stem in
   -#- or -e- (including verbs with an infinitive in -či) also add the ending -en directly to the final consonant of the stem
   but without alternation (the first example
   being an exception).

pêči	~ pečèn	'baked' [note!]
plêsti	~ pletèn	'knitted'
prenêsti	~ prenesèn	'transferred'

vídeti	~	*víden*	'visible'
želéti	~	*želèn*	'desired'

3. The ending -t occurs in a limited number of verbs in which the infinitive ending -ti is preceded by -i-, -e- or -u- and whose present tense has the ending -em or -jem (as opposed to -im) in the lst person singular.

razbíti	~	*razbíjem*	~	*razbít*	'broken'
skríti	~	*skríjem*	~	*skrít*	'hidden'
obúti	~	*obújem*	~	*obút*	'shod'
začéti	~	*začnèm*	~	*začét*	'begun'

SPECIAL CONJUGATIONS

Listed below are the conjugations for several very common verbs in Slovene. Each of them has its own special features, and the student is advised to learn each verb individually:

bíti 'to be'

	present	*negated*	*future*
singular			
1.	sèm	nísem	bóm*
2.	sì	nísi	bóš
3.	jè	ní	bó
dual			
1.	svà	nísva	bóva
2. - 3.	stà	nísta	bósta
plural			
1.	smò	nísmo	bómo
2.	stè	níste	bóste
3.	sò	níso	bódo
-l participle	bíl, bilà, bilò, bilì		
imperative	bódi		

* In addition, one may also encounter the more archaic forms **bódem, bódeš, bóde, bódeva, bódeta, bódemo, bódete, bódejo** as well as the colloquial third person plural future: **bójo.**

	jésti	*dáti*	*védeti*	*íti*
	'to eat'	'to give'	'to know'	'to go'

singular

1.	jém	dám	vém	grém
2.	jéš	dáš	véš	gréš
3.	jé	dá	vé	gré

dual

1.	jéva	dáva	véva	gréva
2. - 3.	jésta	dásta	vésta	grésta

plural

1.	jémo	dámo	vémo	grémo
2.	jéste	dáste	véste	gréste
3.	jéjo	dájo	véjo	grêjo
	or	or	or	or
	jedò	dadó	vedó	gredó

-l participle

jédel/jédla   dál/dála   védel/védela   šèl/šlà

or

jèl/jéla

imperative

jèj   dàj   védi   pójdi

The followings verbs also display pecu-
liarities in their conjugations, and two of them
have special negative forms as well:

	iméti	*hotéti*	*môči*
	'to have'	'to want'	'to be able'

singular

1.	imám (nímam)	hóčem* (nóćem)	mórem
2.	imáš (nímaš)	hóčeš (nóćeš)	móreš
3.	imá (níma)	hóče (nóče)	móre

dual

1.	imáva (nímava)	hóčeva (nóčeva)	móreva
2. - 3.	imáta (nímata)	hóčeta (nóčeta)	móreta

plural

1.	imámo (nímamo)	hóčemo (nóčemo)	móremo
2.	imáte (nímate)	hóčete (nóčete)	mórete
3.	imájo (nímajo)	hóčejo (nóčejo)	mórejo

-l participle

imèl/iméla   hôtel/hotéla   mógel/môgla

imperative

imèj   hôti   --------

* In addition, one may also encounter the non-
  standard colloquial short forms čèm, čès, čè,
  čèva, čèta, čèmo, čète, čèjo.

  [NOTE: Two additional special imperatives:
         poglej from pogledati 'to look (at)'
         vzêmi from vzéti 'to take'.]

COMMENTS ON THE USE OF ASPECTS IN SLOVENE

        As noted earlier, verbs in Slovene come
in pairs, one partner of which is **imperfective**
and one **perfective**. These **aspects** may occur in
any of the tenses. Perfective verbs used in the
present tense, however, often imply an intended
future action (see examples on pp. 93-94). Verbs
in the imperfective aspect denote actions which
are unlimited and which may express one or more
of the following ideas: an action in progress
for some length of time, an action which is repeated or habitual (i.e. occurs frequently), or
an action which is not yet completed. Perfective
verbs, on the other hand, denote actions which
are limited and which have a single termination,
i.e. the beginning or end of an action, or an
action which is instantaneous, momentary or whose
conclusion is expected or foreseen. There are a
few verbs which occur in one or the other aspect
only, a few which are biaspectual, but the typi-
cal verb in Slovene is paired by aspect.
        An unprefixed imperfective verb is
considered the basic form of a verb. Its perfective partner is typically formed from it by the
addition of a prefix. For example, the verb
pisáti 'to write' in its prefixed form **napisáti**
means 'to finish writing'. Among the commonly
used verbal prefixes we find the following:
        do-, iz-, na-, o/ob-, od-, po-,
        pod-, pre-, pred-, pri-, pro-,
        raz-, s-, u-, v-, vz-, z-, za-
Many of the preceding prefixes are derived
from prepositions (compare the lists appearing
on pp. 60-64). Some of these prefixes carry more
than one meaning. The learner will come to recognize them and their meanings with greater

familiarity with the language. In addition to its basic prefixed form **napisáti**, the verb **pisáti** is found in the prefixed perfective forms listed below. [Note: The verb **pisati** and its prefixed forms may be correctly used with the stress on the -a- or -i-, e.g. pisáti OR písati.]

    izpisáti   *'to copy out'*
       *[to write a text **out of** another]*
    opisáti   *'to describe'*
       *[to write **about**]*
    odpisáti   *'to reply in writing'*
       *[to write **from** X to Y]*
    popisáti   *'to inventory'*
       *[to write **bits of** information]*
    podpisáti   *'to sign'*
       *[to write **under**, at the bottom of]*
    prepisáti   *'to copy'*
       *[to transfer **across** in writing]*
    predpisáti *'to prescribe'*
       *[to write **in front of**]*
    pripisáti   *'to annotate'*
       *[to **attach** something in writing]*
    razpisáti   *'to invite application'*
       *[to write **about detailing**]*
    spisáti   *'to compose'*
       *[to put **together** in writing]*
    zapisáti   *'to jot down'*
       [the writing process is done and over,
         *i.e. it is **behind** you]*

     In addition to prefixation, there are other ways in which pairs of imperfective/perfective verbs are formed in Slovene. In many cases verbs display a change within the root or have suffixes in order to distinguish aspect:

imperfective	perfective	
dobívati	*dobíti*	*'to get'*
kupováti	*kupíti*	*'to buy/shop'*
obráčati	*obrníti*	*'to turn'*
odlóčati	*odločíti*	*'to decide'*
ográžati	*ogrozíti*	*'to threaten'*
ostájati	*ostáti*	*'to stay'*
pozdrávljati	*pozdráviti*	*'to greet'*
prežívljati	*preživéti*	*'to spend time'*

uréjati	*uredíti*	'to put in order'
zapisováti	*zapisáti*	'to jot down'
zbírati	*zbráti*	'to gather'

In a limited number of cases an entirely different root is used to form a pair of imperfective/perfective verbs, e.g. **govoríti** 'to speak' ~ **rêči** 'to say' and **jemáti** 'to take' ~ **vzéti** 'to take'.

Sentences with imperfective and perfective verbs:
Imperfective:
Nína je pisála písmo.
    'Nina was writing a letter.'
Grém nakupovát v trgovíno.
    'I'm going shopping.'
Káj boš délal?
    'What will you be doing?'
Lahkó pláčam.
    'I can pay.'
Ne odpíraj tújih písem!
    'Don't open other people's mail!'
Zdàj ga podpisújem.
    'I'm signing it now.'
Ali ne mórete gradíti?
    'Can't you build?'
Cestítali so drúg drúgemu.
    'They congratulated one another.'
Olga ne bêre velíko.
    'Olga doesn't read much.'
Níma smísla čákati.
    'There's no sense in waiting.'
Kóliko čása stojí vlák?
    'How long does the train stay (here)?'
Tó mi boš pláčal!
    'You'll pay (me) for that!'
Kdór ljúbi, tá kaznúje.
    'Spare the rod and spoil the child.'
    (lit.= 'He who loves, that one punishes.')

Perfective:
Nína je napisála písmo.
    'Nina finished writing the letter.'
Knjígo grém kúpit.
    'I'm going to buy a book.'

Jóže je poglédal revíje.
  'Joe looked at the magazines.'
Tréba je/bo podpisáti formulár.
  'The form has to be signed.'
Prídem zjútraj.
  'I'm coming (shall come) in the morning.'
Sóla se začnè 1. októbra.
  'School opens (will begin) on Oct. 1.'
Razbesnèl se je nad menój.
  'He blew up at me.'
Zberíte se!
  'Pull yourself together!'
Narédil sem se, kot da sem jézen.
  'I pretended to be angry.'
Obíščite me jútri.
  'Visit me tomorrow.'
Káj je postàl on?
  'What has become of him?'
Vráta se níso hotéla odpréti.
  'The door wouldn't [=didn't want to] open.'
Ostánete dólgo v Slovéniji?
  'Will you (do you intend to) stay long in
  Slovenia?'

[NOTE: Students who undertake the study of Slovene already knowing another Slavic language should pay particular attention to the use of aspects. Slovene, like Serbo-Croatian, allows the use of the perfective aspect in the present tense. Russian, on the other hand, restricts the use of the perfective aspect to verbal actions in the past and future denoting actions already completed or whose termination is foreseen. The perfective may not be used for a present tense action in Russian.]

TENSE SEQUENCE IN SLOVENE

The learner is cautioned to take note of the sequence of verbal tenses in compound sentences when translating from or into Slovene. There are significant differences between English and Slovene in many cases. Compare, for instance, the following sentences and their translations:

Rékel je, da o tém ničésar ne vé.
'He **said** that he **didn't know** anything
about it.'

Analysis: Whereas both verbs in English occur
in the past tense, the sequence in Slovene is
different.While the first verb is in the past
tense, the second is in the present tense,i.e.
there is something that the speaker **does not
know** at the time he **spoke.**

Lahkó mu oménim tvôje težáve, ko ga bom vídel.
'I **can** mention your difficulties to him
when I **see** him.'

Analysis: In the English translation the verbs
occur in the present tense. (One might also
say 'I'll mention', i.e. future tense.) In
Slovene the first verb is in the perfective
present with an implication of a future act,
and it refers to a specific act, while the
second verb occurs in the imperfective future
without specifying when it is that 'I will be
seeing him'.

Ko boš dóbil tó písmo, bóm že v Berlínu.
'When you **get** that letter I'll already
be in Berlin.'

Analysis: Similar to the preceding sentence,
English uses the present tense in order to
suggest a future action in the first clause,
while in Slovene the future is used. In the
second clause both languages use the future.

Tóne ní védel, ali še živí môja máti.
'Tone **did not know** whether (or not)
my mother **was** still **alive.**'

Analysis: As in the first example English places
both verbs in the past tense creating an ambiguous statement concerning the state of
health of the speaker's mother. In Slovene
the verb of the first clause records an action in the past. Whether or not the mother
of the speaker **is alive** at the time the discussion takes place is a fact of which Tone
was unaware.

Úpal je, da bo ujél zádnji ávtobus próti
   dómu.
   'He hoped that he **would catch** the last bus
   home.'

Analysis: In English 'would' is used in place of
   'will' in compound sentences such as the preceding one. The use of 'would' in such a case
   is not related to the conditional mood discussed earlier. The question here is not one
   of conditions or potential events, rather the
   person **was** thinking and **hoping** at that time
   'I will catch the bus'. Compare the preceding
   to the sentence on p. 83 Če bi védel, bi ti
   povédal. 'If I knew / were to know (but I do
   not), I would tell you (but I can't, since I
   do not know)' in which conditions would have
   to be fulfilled in order for both events to
   occur.

Otròk ní védel, káj se z njím godí.
   'The child **didn't know** what **was**
   happening to him.'
Otròk ní védel, káj se je z njím godílo.
   'The child **didn't know** what **had**
   happened to him.'
Analysis: The first sentence above is like the
   first example in this group. English uses the
   past tense for both clauses, while in Slovene
   it is clear that at the time the action **is**
   taking place, the child **did** **not know** its
   meaning. In the second sentence the child **did**
   not know the meaning of an incident which
   took place at an earlier time.

VERBS WITH THE REFLEXIVE PRONOUNS SE AND SI

   The short forms (clitics) of the reflexive
pronoun sêbe 'oneself', accusative **se** and dative
si (see p. 47), may be used in combination with
a large number of verbs. The presence of the
pronoun produces a variety of different meanings.

Uses of the accusative reflexive pronoun se:

1. When used with transitive verbs, the presence of **se** denotes an action directed back to the subject, e.g.
   Máma umíva otrôka.
      'Mother washes the child.'
              vs.
   Máma se umíva.
      'Mother washes herself.'
   The preceding category includes such verbs as:
   bríti se   'to shave (oneself)'
   obláčiti se   'to dress (oneself)'
   práskati se   'to scratch (oneself)'

2. The use of **se** with a transitive verb often serves to create a passive meaning for the verb, e.g.
   Težkó ga je prepríčati.
     'It's hard to convince him.'
                  vs.
   Prepríčal sem se na lástne očí.
     'I saw it with my own eyes.'
     (i.e. 'I was convinced by my own eyes.')
   Likewise:
   pêči se   'to be baked'
   raníti se   'to be wounded'
   uporábljati se   'to be used'

3. The use of **se** may signify a reciprocal action between two or more persons, e.g.
   Ljúbim Níno.
      'I love Nina.' [transitive verb]
              vs.
   Onádva sta se ljubíla.
      'They loved one another.'
   Likewise:
   pozdrávljati se
      'to exchange mutual greetings'
   razuméti se
      'to understand one another'
   sréčati se
      'to meet one another'

razíti se
   'to separate/go one's way'

4. There are verbs with which the reflexive
   pronoun **se** must **always** be used. They are
   intransitive. (The **se** carries with it no
   inherent self directed, passive or reciprocal meaning):
   Ne **bójte se**! (from **báti se**)
      'Don't be afraid!'
   Likewise:
   čúditi se   'to wonder'
   jókati se   'to cry'
   počutíti se   'to feel'
   smejáti se   'to laugh'
   spómniti se   'to remember'

5. Some verbs are combined with **se** in the
   third person singular to convey impersonal
   constructions, i.e. those in which the subject is not named:
   Ne **vé se, kdáj bodo prišlì.**
      'Nobody knows when they will arrive.'
      (i.e. 'It is not known...)
                     vs.
   Jàz tó vém. 'I know that.'
   Likewise:
   govorí se   'it is rumored'
   mísli se   'it is thought'
   slíši se   '(something) is heard'

   The dative reflexive **si** pronoun denotes
an action performed for the benefit of the
subject of the verb. Only a few verbs are
obligatorily used with **si**. There is a growing
preference for the **se** form. For instance, one
finds both **úpati si** and **úpati se** 'to dare' and
oddahníti si and **oddahníti se** 'to recover'.
Verbs accompanied by **si** in common use include:
      mísliti si   'to imagine'
      ogledováti si   'to sightsee'
      pomagáti si   'to help oneself'/'to
                          find a way'
      zapómniti si   'to keep in mind'
      želéti si   'to wish for oneself'

NOTES ON VERBAL STRESS

1. (a) As stated earlier Slovene recognizes three basic stress patterns: A and B which are non-mobile on the root and ending respectively; a mobile C stress pattern. The vast majority of Slovene verbs have a non-mobile A pattern in which the stress falls on the root in the infinitive, present tense, imperative, participle in -l, supine and past participle. It includes such common verbs as:

mísliti	'to think'
dvígniti	'to raise'
rézati	'to cut'
délati	'to work'
sésti	'to sit down'
vérovati	'to believe'
mériti	'to measure'

(b) The number of verbs which display a non-mobile B stress pattern is considerably smaller. It such verbs the stress falls on the final vowel of the stem before the ending is added in the same forms enumerated above. Note, however, that in the basic form of the imperative (the second person singular) of those verbs which take -i, that -i cannot be stressed, while it is stressed in other forms of the imperative.

Infinitive/1st person	Imperative	
končáti/končám	*končàj/končájte*	'to end'
kupováti/kupújem	*kupúj/kupújte*	'to buy'
grešíti/greším	*grêši/grešíte*	'to sin'
besnéti/besním	*bêsni/besníte*	'to rage'
govoríti/govorím	*govôri/govoríte*	'to speak'

2. In those verbs which display a mobile C stress pattern there is a retraction (moving back) of the stress by one syllable in the present tense, in basic form of the imperative (the second person singular) and in the masculine singular of the descriptive participle in -l.

(infinitive, followed by the 1st person,
singular and plural imperatives, and the
masculine and feminine participle in -l)

'to defend'   braníti ~ bránim ~
    bráni/braníte ~ bránil / braníla
'to set out'   kreníti ~ krénem ~
    krêni/kreníte ~ krênil / kreníla
'to be silent'   molčáti ~ molčím ~
    mólči/molčíte ~ mólčal / molčála
'to comb'   česáti ~ čéšem ~
    čêši/česíte ~ čêsal / česála
'to say'   rêči ~ rêčem ~
    rêci/recíte ~ rékel / rêkla
'to read'   bráti ~ bêrem ~
    bêri/beríte ~ brál / brála

NOTE: The verbs rêči and bráti are included
above even though they are stressed on the
first syllable in the infinitive and present
tense. The shift is seen in the second person
plural of the imperative. Further, the form
molčím with a stressed ending on all forms of
the present tense is an exception. A number
of other verbs in common use also display the
same stress irregularity. They include:
    'to run' bežáti ~ bežím
    'to hold' držáti ~ držím
    'to lie' ležáti ~ ležím and others.

3. Stress for participles:
    a.) Stress for the participle in -l is
    covered in notes 1. and 2. above.

    b.) The present adverbial participle in -e
    is always stressed on the final syllable,
    e.g. molčé and vedé, and those in -je are
    stressed on the syllable immediately pre-
    ceding, e.g. kupováje and deláje.

    c.) The past adverbial participle ending in
    -vši / -ši is stressed on the next to last
    syllable (the final vowel of the stem of the
    infinitive), e.g.
        končávši and dvignívši.

d.) The present adjectival participle in -č
is always stressed on the final syllable,
e.g. delajóč and misléč.

e.) The stress of the past adjectival participle normally coincides with the stress of
the first person singular, e.g.
   kúpim ~ kúpljen and ránim ~ ránjen.

MISCELLANEOUS NOTES AND SOME SPECIAL PROBLEMS OF SYNTAX AND GRAMMAR

THE USE OF THE DUAL IN SLOVENE

Slovene recognizes three numbers for nominal, pronominal and adjectival declensions, as well as for verbal conjugations: singular, dual and plural. The dual in Slovene, with one exception, is unique among the Slavic languages and indeed among the major languages of Europe. It is a very old category which had fallen into partial disuse over time. Its continued use, however, was assured in the nineteenth century when Contemporary Standard Slovene was codified, i.e. standardized, becoming the language now used by educated Slovenes and as the literary norm in the mass media and the arts. One hears the dual used in everyday speech on the streets of Ljubljana, while its use in the dialects is less consistent.

As seen in the various charts of declensions presented throughout this text, the dual does not have a complete set of forms for all cases in the nominal and adjectival declensions as do the singular and plural numbers. The nominative and accusative cases are the same, as are the dative and instrumental. The genitive and locative cases coincide with the same case forms of the plural. The dual forms for pronouns is somewhat more developed. In verbal conjugation there is a set of forms for the first person, while the second and third persons share the same form.

The general rule is that the dual is used when referring to two persons or objects. In the case of nouns, the numeral for 'two' or 'both' must appear in order for the dual form to be used. Once having been stated in a given situation, the number need not be mentioned again. (See the first two examples below.) For verbs it is sufficient for the number two to be implied:

Živéla sta dvá bráta.
   'There (once) lived two brothers.'
Bráta sta hodíla v Máribor.
   'The (two) brothers went to Maribor.'
Tù sta dvá čévlja.
   'There are two shoes here.'
Hódiva na délo.
   'We (two) go to work.'
Bilà sva v Zágrebu.
   'We (two) were in Zagreb.'

When parts of the body (eyes, eyebrows, ears, arms, legs, knees, wings, etc.) or objects which normally come in pairs (such as sleeves, socks, gloves, earmuffs) are not specifically referred to by number, the **plural** is used:

Ušésa me bolé.	'My ears ache.'
Očí so mu goréle.	'His eyes burned.'
Imám hládne róke.	'I have cold hands.'
Rokavíce sem pozábil.	'I forgot my gloves.'

but

dvé nógi, môji dvé očési
   'two feet', 'my two eyes'
Sprejél ponúdbo z obéma rókama.
   'He jumped at the offer.' [= 'He accepted the offer with both hands.']
Izgubíla je obé rokavíci.
   'She lost both gloves.'
Oslepèl je na obé očési.
   'He became blind in both eyes.'

ANIMATE VS. INANIMATE

There are times in Slovene when the speaker must choose between using the accusative or genitive case of a noun depending upon whether that noun refers to a person or animal, i.e. it is **animate**, or to an **inanimate** object. The choice arises in connection with transitive verbs requiring a direct object in the accusative case, as well as with prepositions which govern the accusative case. Further, only **masculine nouns in the singular** are affected by this rule. The accusative case ending for masculine nouns in the singular is identical with

either the nominative or the genitive case,
while in the dual and plural the nominative,
genitive and accusative cases of masculine nouns
each have different endings. Compare the accusative endings for the words **pótnik** 'traveller'
and **móst** 'bridge' on p. 26. Neuter nouns are not
affected, since virtually all of them refer to
inanimate objects (exceptions: **déte** 'child' and
deklè 'girl').

Nor are feminine nouns affected, since
feminine declensions in most cases distinguish
between the nominative, genitive and accusative
cases in the singular, dual and plural. (Feminine nouns ending in a consonant such as **miš**
'mouse' are an exception. (See p. 27.)

The general rule states that the accusative ending for masculine nouns in the singular
is **-a**, i.e. the same as the genitive ending, if
the point of reference is animate (a living
being, person or an animal) and the zero ending
(**-#**) if it is inanimate (a non-living object),
i.e. the same as the nominative case.

Examples

Imám sína.
  'I have a son.'
Imám účbenik.
  'I have a textbook.'
Stárši skrbíjo za otrôka.
  'Parents care for their child.'
Skríli so se za zíd.
  'They hid behind the wall.'
vs.
Imám sinóve.
  'I have sons.'
Imám účbenike.
  'I have textbooks.'
Stárši skrbíjo za otróke.
  'Parents care for their children.'
Skríli so se za zidôve.
  'They hid behind the walls.'

There are some important exceptions to the
above rule. Certain groups of nouns behave as
animates, even though they are not. They include:

1. titles of newspapers referring to a person (**Lóvec**)
2. brands of cars (**fíat**)
3. labels of wines (**vipávec**)
4. names of playing cards (**ás, pík**)
5. mushrooms (**gobàn**)
6. names of diseases (**ràk**)
7. planets (**Júpiter**)
8. sports clubs referring to a person (**Slován**)
9. a misc. group of nouns including the words:
   (a)   **dúh**   'soul'
   (b)   words meaning 'dead person'/'corpse'/ 'cadaver' **mrlìč, mrtvák, mŕtvec**

DOUBLE NEGATIVES

Slovene, like many other European languages, employs the rule of double negation. Thus, the presence of a pronoun or adverb in **ni-** requires that the verb be negated as well, i.e.:

Kdór nìč ne tvéga, nìč níma.
    'Nothing ventured, nothing gained.'
    ['He who risks nothing has nothing.']
Nikómur nísem ničésar rékel.
    'I did not say anything to anybody.'
Nikógar nísem vídel.
    'I didn't see anybody.'
Nikóli nikjér ga ne nájdeš.
    'You can never find him anywhere.'
Téga nikár ne délaj!
    'Be sure not to do that.'

SPECIAL USES OF THE GENITIVE CASE

In addition to the use of the genitive case with numerals above 5 (see p. 57), there are a number of other special constructions requiring the genitive. They are outlined below.

1. GENITIVE OF NEGATION

In the examples used above under **double negatives** we see the use of the genitive of negation in the words **ničésar, nikógar** and **téga**.

When transitive verbs which take a direct object
in the accusative case are negated, the accusative case is normally replaced by the genitive
case in all numbers:

Poznám hotél/hotéle.
   'I know the hotel/hotels.'
Ne poznám hotéla/hotélov
   'I don't know the hotel/hotels.'
Mírko imá knjígo/knjíge.
   'Mirko has the book/books.'
Mírko níma knjíge/knjíg.
   'Mirko doesn't have the book/books.'
Poglédal sem danášnjo póšto.
   'I saw today's mail.'
Nísem poglédal danášnje póšte.
   'I didn't see today's mail.'
Nísmo vídeli tvójega kolésa.
   'We didn't see your bike.'
Nísmo vídeli váših kolés.
   'We didn't see your bikes.'
Ne mórete telefonírati, če nímate žetónov.
   'You can't call, if you don't have tokens.'

Note also the following pair of sentences. In the first one the subject occurs in
the nominative case as expected. In the second
one the subject is in the genitive case due to
the presence of a negated form of the verb 'to
be' (see also pp. 33-34, 121-122 for other
similar examples):

Oče je domá.   'Father is home.'
Očéta ní domá.   'Father is not home.'

2. GENITIVE OF QUANTITY

The following words indicate quantity and
require the use of the genitive:
málo 'little'/'few', **mnógo/velíko** 'much'/'many',
as well as **kàj** 'some'/'any', **nékaj** 'some(thing)'
or 'several' and **nìč** 'nothing', e.g.
málo/mnógo (velíko)/nékaj híš
   'a few/many/several houses'
málo/mnógo/nékaj zanimívega
   'little/much/something of interest'

and

velíko sréče!	'lots of luck!'
málo prijáteljev	'(a) few friends'
mnógo čása	'lots of time'
nékaj drobíža	'some change'
še kaj drúgega	'something else'
nìč húdega	'nothing bad'

The word **kóliko** 'how much / many' also requires the use of the genitive case in that it refers to quantity:

Kóliko hotélov je v Ljubljáni?
    'How many hotels are there in Ljubljana?'
Kóliko denárja imáte?
    'How much money do you have?'

The genitive case may also be used if one wishes to express an idea of **approximation** with the word **kàk**:

Kóliko hotélov?
    'How many hotels?'
Kàkih pét / desét / dvájset.
    'Some five / ten / twenty.'

and

Kóliko je stára njegóva žêna?
    'How old is his wife?'
Kàkih pétdeset.
    'About fifty.'

Under the category of quantity we may also include the **partitive genitive**. If part of something, as opposed to the whole of it, is desired, then the genitive is used:

Dàj mi / vzê mi si čája / krúha / síra.
    'Give me / take (for yourself) **some** tea
    / bread / cheese.'
                    vs.
Dàj mi / vzêmi si čáj / krúh / sír.
    'Give me/take (for yourself) **the** tea
    / bread / cheese.'

3. **EXCEPTIONAL USE OF ADJECTIVES AND
    PRONOUNS IN THE GENITIVE CASE**

Note the following use of feminine nouns modified by adjectives and pronouns declined like adjectives in the accusative case in the sentences which follow:

Jàz imám svôjo knjígo.
  'I have my book.'
Vzêmi še ti svôjo.
  'Take yours also.'
                and
Katéro slívovko hóčete?
  'Which plum brandy do you want?'
Slovénsko.
  'A Slovene one.'

    In the case of phrases in which the adjective or pronoun modifies an **omitted** masculine or neuter noun, however, the adjective or pronoun appears in the genitive case rather than in the expected accusative case:

Jàz imám svój kóvček.
  'I have my suitcase.'
Vzêmi še ti svójega.
  'Take yours also.'
Katéri klobúk hóčete?
  'Which hat do you want?'
Téga ali ónega?
  'This one or that one?'
Katéro víno naj prinêsem?
  'Which wine should I bring?'
Prinesíte lánskega / rdéčega.
  'Bring last year's' / 'a red one.'
[See also example on p. 52.]

SOME SPECIAL MODAL VERBS AND EXPRESSIONS

    There are special vocabulary items and/or syntactic rules for constructing sentences in Slovene with words which correspond to English 'can' / 'may', 'to be allowed', 'must', 'it is necessary' and 'prefer' / 'like'.

môči 'can' / 'may'

    The verb môči in Slovene with its present tense **mórem, móreš**, etc. (see its conjugation on p. 80) has the meaning of 'to be (physically) able(to do something)' / 'to be capable' / 'can'. It is followed by an infinitive:

Mórem samó pohvalíti...
  'I can only praise....'

Dánes ne mórem délati.
   'I cannot work today.'
Na izpítu se nikákor nisem mógel zbráti.
   *'I couldn't concentrate at all at
    the exam.'*
Stóril bom, kár bom nájveč mógel.
   'I'll do the best (most) that I can.'

When one wishes, however, to convey the
meaning of 'can' in the sense of 'may' (permission granted)/'might' in Slovene, the word **lahkó**
(literally 'easily') plus a finite form of the
verb is used:

Lahkó vstópim?
   'Can/may I come in?'
Lahkó me poklíčete, kàdar kóli želíte.
   'You can/may call me whenever you wish.'
Lahkó tó bêreš?
   'Can you read this?'
Lahkó, da je pozábil.
   'He might have forgotten.'

In the event of a negative reply, the word
lahko is not used. The speaker reverts to the
verb **móči** if there is some physical hinderance
(for permission denied, see **sméti** below):

Ne mórete še vstopíti.
   *'You can't come in yet.' [Because, e.g. the
    floors are still wet.]*
Téga ne móreš bráti.
   *'You can't read this.' [Because, e.g.:
    I'm reading it . /It's too difficult.
    / It's in a foreign language. See also
    example under sméti.]*
Ne móreš takó govoríti s staréjšimi od sêbe.
   *'You can not speak to your elders like
    that.' [You did, and you are being re-
    proached for having done so. See also
    final example under sméti.]*

sméti 'to be allowed'

The verb **sméti** has the meaning 'to be
allowed' or 'to be permitted, i.e. a more emphatic granting or denying of permission than in
the 'can'/'may' constructions above:

Ali smém vprašáti...?
   'Am I allowed to ask...?'
Ali smém telefonírati od vàs?
   'Am I allowed to use your telephone?'
Túkaj se ne smé kadíti.
   'Smoking is forbidden here.'
Ona ne smé iz híše.
   'She's not allowed out.'
Ne méš téga bráti.
   'You are not allowed to read this.'
Ne méš takó govoríti s staréjšimi od sêbe.
   'You are not allowed (may not) to talk to
     your elders like that.' [A rule is stated
     without a strong reproach being issued.]

mórati 'must' / 'should'

     The verb **mórati** means 'must' / 'should'
/ 'ought' / 'to have to'. [**Note**: Be careful not
to confuse its present tense conjugation with
that of **môči**!] **Mórati**, like **môči**, belongs to a
limited group of verbs which require an infinitive complement. The infinitive may be deleted
(but it remains implied) with verbs of motion:
Móraš domóv/k zdravníku.
   'You must / should / ought / have to go
     home / go see a doctor.'
Tó knjígo mórate prebráti.
   'You must read this book.'
Móral je umréti.
   'He was doomed to die.'

tréba 'it is necessary'

     A construction with the word **tréba** ex-
presses the concept 'it is necessary'('needed')
as in the following examples:
Tó je tréba storíti.
   'It is necessary to do this.'
Ní tréba délati.
   'It's not necessary to work.'
Káj je še tréba?
   'What else is needed?'
Ní mi tréba tvôjega denárja.
   'I don't need your money.'

iméti ràd 'prefer' / 'like'

The adjective ràd (see p. 39) and its comparative rájši/ráje (literally 'glad'/'more gladly') or the superlative with naj- combined with the verb iméti 'to have' in Slovene corresponds to the English meanings: 'to prefer', 'to like' ('to love' when speaking about a person), 'rather'/ 'sooner', 'to be willing'. When used with verbs other than iméti its use is adverbial and its meaning closer to the original 'gladly'. Note its use in the following sentences:

Ràd imám láhka vína.
'I like light wines.'
Rádi imájo šáh.
'They like (to play) chess.'
Najrájši/najráje imám čaj.
'I'd much rather have tea.'
Péter zeló neràd odgovárja na písma.
'Peter hates (really prefers not) to
answer letters.'
Ali se ráda učíš slovénščino?
'Do you like studying Slovene?'
Jóže bi rájši/ráje ostál v Ljubljáni.
'Joe would prefer to stay in Ljubljana.'
Nína bi ráje odpotovála, kot pa da bi
drúžila z máno!
'Nina would sooner leave than join me!'
Mí bi ráje šlì péš.
'We'd prefer to walk (go by foot).'

VERBS OF MOTION AND CASE REQUIREMENTS

In Slovene there are many verbs which fall into a category known as verbs of motion. Such verbs suggest the movement of a person or object from one location to another. The prepositions which follow such verbs will require the noun to be in the accusative case, while the same prepositions used with verbs indicating a stationary position will be used with a case other than accusative. [Review prepositions on pp. 60-64.] There are also several paired adverbs which designate place as opposed to movement including:

place		motion		
kjé	'where'	kám/kód	'where'	['whither']
túkaj	'here'	sèm	'here'	['hither']
tàm	'there'	tjà	'there'	['thither']

Compare the following sentences:

Kjé si bíl?   *'Where were you?'*
Bíl sem v Ljubljáni. *'I was in Ljubljana.'*
[The sentences above indicate a stationary
 location, not movement, and **v** takes the
 locative case.]

as opposed to

Kám gréš?   *'Where are you going?'*
Grém v Ljubljáno. *'I'm going to Ljubljana.'*
[These sentences indicate movement/express
 direction to a place, and **v** takes the
 accusative case.]

likewise

Hódiva na délo.
   'We (two) go to work.'
Mídva sva bilà na délu.
   'We (two) were at work.'
Kdó je pádel v vôdo?
   'Who fell into the water?'
Pomorščák je v vôdi.
   'A sailor is in the water.'
Sédli smo pod drevó.
   'We sat down under the tree.'
Ležáli smo pod drevésom.
   'We were lying under the tree.'
Peljíte ga v môjo sôbo!
   'Take him into my room!'
Júrij léta sèm in tjà.
   'Jurij is running (flying) here and there.'
Nêsi tó písmo na pôšto!
   'Take this letter to the post office!'

Verbs of motion include such verbs as:

bežáti	'to run'
íti	'to go'
hodíti	'to walk'
gnáti	'to impel'
létati/letéti	'to fly'
nosíti/nêsti	'to carry'
plávati	'to swim'/'to sail'

vodíti/vêsti	*'to lead'*
vozíti	*'to drive'*
	AND
léči	*'to lie down'*
peljáti	*'to take'*
položíti	*'to place (lying)'*
sésti	*'to sit down'*
postáviti	*'to place (standing)'*
vréči	*'to throw'*

Many of the verbs in the preceding list have prefixed and related forms derived from them which are part of the inventory of verbs of motion.

TIME EXPRESSIONS

Slovene, like any language, has its own special way of phrasing time expressions, dates and telling age. Age and time expressions employ cardinal numbers, while dates use ordinals (see pp. 54-55). They are summarized below.

1. **TELLING AGE**: The formula for designating age is a simple one:
   Kóliko je stàr Jóže/stára Nína?
        'How old is Joe/Nina?'
   Òn/Ona je stàr/stára... 'He/She is...

êno léto	1
dvé léti	2
trí/štíri léta	3/4
pét lét	5
ênaindvájset lét	21
dváintridéset lét	32
pétinšéstdeset lét.	65 years old.'

   [Refer to pp. 56-57 for case requirements.]
   In order to state approximation of age, one may use the following constructions:
   Blíža se k pétdesetim.
        'He/she is approaching his/her fifties.'
   je v zgódnjih/pôznih trídesetih
        'in one's early/late thirties'

2. **TELLING TIME**: There are often several ways to state the same time expression in Slovene. Compare the various possibilities offered below. The learner is also reminded that the 24 hour clock is used in most official areas of life, so that 14 hrs. is 2 p.m. and 20 hrs. is 8 p.m., etc. Further, in written Slovene a period(decimal point) is used to separate the hour and minute(s) rather than a colon as is done in English.
   Kóliko je úra? 'What time is it?'
   Úra je... 'It is...'

1:00	êna [**nom.**]
2:00	dvé
3:00	trí
10:00	desét

```
12:30    pôl ênih (or êne) [pol+gen.]
1:30     pôl dvéh
2:30     pôl tréh
9:30     pôl desêtih
12:15    četŕt na êno/êna [na+acc.]
1:15     četŕt na dvé
2:15     četŕt na trí
9:15     četŕt na desét
12:45    trí četŕt na êno/êna
1:45     trí četŕt na dvé
2:45     trí četŕt na trí
9:45     trí četŕt na desét
              OR
1:15     Ura je êna in pétnajst (minút).
         Ura je četŕt čez êno. [čez+acc.]
1:30     Ura je êna in trídeset (minút).
1:45     Ura je êna in pétinštírideset.
         Čez pétnajst bo dvé.
         Ura je pétnajst do dvéh. [do+gen.]
              PLUS
1:01     Ura je êna minúta čez êno.
1:02     dvé minúti čez êno.
1:05     pét minút čez êno.
              ALSO
1:07     Ura je êna in sédem minút.
1:40     dvájset minút do dvéh
2:55     Čez pét minút bo trí.
2:57     Čez trí minúte bo trí.
2:59     Čez êno minúto bo trí.
              OR
2:55     pét minút do tréh
3:57     do štírih mánjka (še) trí minúte
4:59     êna minúta do pét
```

```
Kdáj?          'When?'          [ob + loc.]
Ob ênih  OR  ob êni úri         'at 1:00'
Ob dvéh                         'at 2:00'
Ob petnájstih                   'at 3:00 (p.m.)'
Ob pôl desêtih                  'at 9:30'
Ob desêtih in dvájset(minút)    'at 10:20'
```

3. EXPRESSING AMOUNTS OF TIME:

(a) In order to state that an event will take place in a certain period of time, the preposition čez with the accusative case of the number is used:
Jóže bo túkaj čez êno úro / pét úr / èn mésec.
   *'Joe will be here in one / five hour(s) /
   a month.'*

(b) In order to specify the duration of an action, the simple accusative is used, i.e. without a preposition. [**Hint:** If the preposition 'for' in English may be omitted, then no preposition is required in Slovene.]
*Bóris je délal êno úro / dvé úri / pét úr
   / vsò zímo.*
   *'Boris was working (for) one / two / five
   hours / all winter.'*

(c) In order to state the length of time in which an action can be accomplished, **v** plus the locative is used:
*Tó bom narédil v êni úri / dvéh / pétih
   úrah / v ênem tédnu.*
   *'I shall get that done in one / two / five
   hours / in a week.'*

(d) In order to specify that an action is done with a certain frequency, the preposition **na** plus the accusative is used:
*ênkrat na léto / dvákrat na téden / tríkrat
   na minúto*
   *'once a (per) year' / 'twice a week' /
   'three times a minute'*

(e) In order to express time 'before' ('by') which an event occurs, the preposition **do** followed by the genitive case is used:
Prišèl bom k váma / Pri váju bóm do tréh.
   *'I'll get to / be at your place before
   (by) three.'*
Likewise, the prepositions **od....do**, both followed by the genitive case, express the concept 'from.....to':

Mesníca je odpŕta od dvéh do sêdmih.
  'The butcher shop is open from two to
    seven.'

(f) In order to specify the length of time
that a given action is intended to last or
to be in effect, the preposition **za** is used
followed by the accusative case:
Za kóliko dní ste rezervírali sóbo?
  'For how many days did you reserve the
    room?'
Za èn dán/dvá dní.
  'For one/two days.'

4. DATES:

(a) Requesting and stating the current date
may be done by the use of the nominative or
genitive cases:
Katéri dátum/dán je dánes? 'What date is it?'
Dánes je devéti. [nom.] 'Today is the ninth.'
Devéti máj. [nom.]   'May 9th.'
                    OR
Katérega smo dánes?'   'What date is it?'
Dánes smo devétega.[gen.]'Today is the ninth.'
Devétega mája. [gen.]   'May 9th.'

(b) When stating the date on which an event
takes place, the use of the genitive is
obligatory:
Lahkó prídete devétega?
  'Can you come on the ninth?'
Prešéren je umŕl ôsmega fébruarja.
  'Prešeren died on February 8th.'

(c) Dates involving years are stated in the
following way:
Smo tísoč devétsto devétdesetega. [gen.]
  'It is 1990.'
*Rôjen sem (rodíl sem se) tísoč devétsto
    pétdesetega léta. [gen.]*
  'I was born in 1950.'
                    OR
*Rôjen sem léta [gen.] tísoč devétsto
  pétinšéstdeset.*

'I was born in 1965.'
                          AND
Rôjen sem trídesetega mája [gen.] tísoč
    devétsto sédemdesetega.
'I was born on May 30, 1970.'
Prešéren se je rodíl trétjega decêmbra
    tísoč ósemsto.
'Prešeren was born on December 3rd, 1800.'

5. NAMES OF THE DAYS OF THE WEEK:

Katéri dán je dánes?
   'What day (of the week) is it?'
Dánes je ponedéljek.   'Today is Monday.'
      tôrek   Tuesday   sréda   Wednesday
      četŕtek Thursday   pétek   Friday
      sobóta   Saturday   nedélja Sunday
In order to say 'on Monday, Tuesday, Wednes-
day', etc. the preposition **v** is used with the
accusative case:
      v ponedéljek, v tôrek, v srédo...
The plural, 'on Sundays, on Mondays', etc. is
expressed by using the preposition **ob** with
the locative case:
      ob nedéljah, ob ponedéljkih...

6. NAMES OF THE MONTHS: The names of the months
are given below. [Note: months may also be
read by the use of the ordinal numerals in
order 'first' through 'twelfth'. For example,
in European style 2.VII.1701 is to be read as
7/2/1701 in American style. It may be read as
drúgega sêdmega tísoč šedemsto pŕvega léta.]

         jánuar   júlij
         fébruar   avgúst
         márec   septêmber
         apríl   október
         máj   novêmber
         júnij   decêmber
All of the month names are masculine. In
order to say 'in January', 'in March', etc.,
the preposition **v** is used with the locative
case, e.g. **v jánuarju, v márcu.** OR the genitive case may be used, e.g.

Fébruarja je pádlo velíko snegá.
　　'A lot of snow fell in February.'

7. DIVISIONS OF THE DAY:

		'in the...'/'at'
'morning'	*jútro*	*zjútraj/dopóldne*
('good morning'	*dôbro jútro)*	
'day'	*dán*	*podnévi/čez dán*
('good day'	*dóber dán)*	
'evening'	*večér*	*zvečér*
('good evening'	*dóber večér)*	
'night'	*nóč*	*ponôči*
('good night'	*láhko nóč) [note!]*	

note also:

'noon'	*póldan*	*'at noon'*	*opóldne*
'midnight'	*pólnoč*	*'at midnight'*	*opólnoči*
'a.m.'	*dopóldne*	*'p.m.'*	*popóldne*

'today'	*dánes*
'yesterday'	*včéraj*
'tomorrow'	*jútri*
'this morning'	*dávi*
'tonight'	*nocój*
'this evening'	*drévi*

8. THE YEAR AND ITS SEASONS:

'year'	*léto*	
	'this year'	*létos*
	'last year'	*láni*
	'next year'	*drúgo/prihódnje léto*
'month'	*mésec*	
	'this month'	*tá mésec*
	'last month'	*préjšnji mésec*
	'next month'	*drúgi/prihódnji mésec*

'season'	*létni čás*	*'in the...'*
'spring'	*pomlád*	*spomládi*
'summer'	*polétje*	*poléti*
'autumn'	*jesén*	*jeséni*
'winter'	*zíma*	*pozími*

WORD ORDER IN SLOVENE

Word order in Slovene is considered to be **free**. That "freedom", however, is only relative. The meaning which a speaker wishes to convey in a given situation determines the order in which words appear in a sentence. Additionally, word order is closely connected with the imparting of new information and with the overall stress/intonation of the sentence. **Independent** words, a term used here to include nouns, adjectives, adverbs, numerals and verbs, normally occupy a specific position within a sentence. Their position is rather rigidly defined to the extent that if their place in the sentence is changed, or if the intonation of the sentence is changed, the meaning which the speaker intends also changes. Thus, the position which any given word occupies within a sentence determines the effect which the speaker wishes to achieve. **Dependent** words, a term used to include prepositions, conjunctions, negatives, particiles, short form pronouns (clitics) and forms of the verb **bíti** 'to be' (auxiliaries) adhere to a much stricter word order. Explanations provided here are meant to serve only as a general guide to word order in Slovene. To cover all aspects of Slovene word order is beyond the scope of a work such as this, and the student of Slovene is urged to cultivate the habit of careful reading and analysis of new texts from the beginning.

The general principle governing word order in simple or compound **declarative sentences** (and in **commands**) is that information which is given or known (the **theme**) is considered the **least significant** and comes first. It is followed by new information (the **rheme**) and is considered to be of **maximum significance** and is stated in order of its importance. A sentence in Slovene may begin with a noun and its modifiers, if any, as subject. (Many begin with adverbs or prepositional phrases.) A personal pronoun, unless stressed, is normally omitted. Then follows a verb and its complements, adverbial or prepositional modifiers, or perhaps another noun or an adjective:

Nàš Márjan je
  'Our Marjan [subject] is [verb]
     učítelj. a teacher.' [noun]
     mlád. young.' [adjective]
     domá. home.' [adverb]

 Grêgor je písal
  'Gregor [subject] was writing [verb]
  knjígo a book.' [direct object]
  žêni. to his wife.' [indir. obj.]
  trí úre. for three hours.'
  [accusative expression of time]

   Let us examine the sentence **Njegóv stári dèd gré létos v Amériko na obísk.** 'His old grandfather is going to America on a visit this year.' It contains an adverb and two prepositional phrases at the end of the sentence in which the new information (**rheme**), i.e. that of maximum importance, of the sentence is contained. The subject is a given (**theme**) consisting of three words and is of least importance in ther sentence. The fact that he has an old grandfather has apparently already been established as a topic of conversation. It is followed by the verb. The adverb **létos** comes after the verb followed by the prepositional phrases. The adverb and the two prepositional phrases could change places within the sentence, each time creating different results. Here **na obísk** is the final phrase, suggesting that the sentence is in response to the question "For what reason is he going to America?" ('on a visit' – perhaps he has been there earlier on business). Had the adverb **létos** come at the end of the sentence, then the emphasis would have shifted to 'this summer' in response to an implied question "When will he visit America?". If the phrase **v Amériko** had come at the end of the sentence, then the impact would be a response to the question "Where is he going?" ('to America' – as opposed to some other country).

  In the sentence **Nášega máčka že trí dní ni domóv.** 'Our cat hasn't (come) home for three days now.' the noun phrase **nášega máčka** is the subject and appears in the genitive due to the negated verb **ni**. (See pp. 34 and 106 for similar examples.) The word **že** emphasizes the accusative time phrase **trí dní** which follows, and finally the most important piece of information **domóv** tells where it is that the cat has not been.

The least / maximum rule will take precedence over a word order based on parts of speech as can be seen in the following two sentences each consisting of only two words (no pronoun is necessary, the information being supplied by the ending of the verb):

Móram bráti.   'I must **read**.'
('Must' is a given, or presumed, and the under- taking of reading as opposed to some other ac- tion, such as writing or singing, is new.)

Bráti móram.   'I **must** read.'
(You already know that there is reading to be done, and now it is time that it **must** be done, i.e. it cannot be delayed further.)
[**HINT**: The emphasis (stress) in English sen- tences such as the two above will often help to decide the word order in Slovene.]

The least / maximum principle for given vs. new information applies to compound sen- tences such as **Dánes je hladnó, zató ostáneva domá.** [= **Dánes je hladnó. Ostáneva domá.**] 'It's cold today, therefore we're staying home.' There is no subject expressed in the first part of the sentence, and here the adverb **dánes** precedes the verb, which is followed by the word **hladnó**. The clause which follows contains a finite verb form for the first person dual ('the two of us are staying') and an adverb. The new information of maximal significance is 'cold' in the independ- ent clause and '(at) home' in the dependent clause.

The compound sentence **Rêci mu, da je njegóva knjíga pri mêni.** 'Tell him that I have his book.' follows the normal word order. The first part contains an imperative verb and the dative case of the masculine pronoun **on** (who is to be told). The subject pronoun **ti** is absent, as noted above. It is clear from the verbal ending. In the clause which follows, the phrase

njegóva knjíga is the subject of the verb **je**
(see below for placement of the clitic **je**), and
the sentence concludes with a prepositional
phrase (**where** the book is).

The following three sentences further
illustrate the relationship between information
of least and maximum significance and the question of word order:

1. **Na nášem vŕtu je vsè v cvétju.**
2. **Vsè je v cvétju na nášem vŕtu.**
3. **Vsè na nášem vŕtu je v cvétju.**

In each case those elements or units which the
speaker feels are not divisable are grouped
together. The placing of the various elements
tells us what the speaker considers to be information of least or maximum significance.

The sentences might be translated in the
following way:

1. 'In our garden **everything is in bloom.**'
    (We don't have to wait for anything to
    bloom now.)
                WHERE ? + WHAT ? / HOW ?
2. 'Everything is in bloom **in our garden.**'
    (Elsewhere not everything is out yet.)
                WHAT ? / HOW ? + WHERE ?
3. 'Everything in our garden is **in bloom.**'
    (There is nothing that doesn't have a
    flower on it.)
                WHAT ? / WHERE ? + HOW ?

Questions in Slovene are freqently
introduced by interrogatives such as **kjé**
'where', **kám** 'where (to)', **kdó** 'who', **káj**
'what', **kdáj** 'when', **zakáj** 'why', **kakó** 'how',
etc. or by prepositional phrases. They are
usually followed by a verb, then its subject, if
any, and finally by additional information as
required by the question:

Kdáj gré ávtobus?
   'When does the bus leave?'
Kjé je telefónski imeník?
   'Where's the telephone book?'
Kám gréš jútri?
   'Where are you going tomorow?'
Kdó je v híši?
   'Who is in the house?'

Káj je tó?
   'What's that?'
Kjé si dóbil té knjíge?
   'Where did you get those books?'
Kakó je tó móžno?
   'How is that possible?'
Od kód prihájaš?
   'Where are you coming from?'
S katérim vlákom se boš peljála?
   'Which train will you take?'
Na katére naslóve naj pǒšljem tó
  sporočílo?
   'To which addresses should I send
   this information?'

    In the absence of an interrogative pronoun, adverb or prepositional phrase as in the preceding questions, the word ali (un-stressed) is used to introduce explicit questions to which the answer 'yes' or 'no' is required, even in an embedded question as seen in the last example immediately below:

Ali véš, kakó se imenúje tísta gôra?
  'Do you know what the name of that
  mountain is?'
Ali je domá?
  'Is he/she home?'
Ali govoríte slovénsko?
  'Do you speak Slovene?'
Ni mi povédal, ali se res ločúje.
  'He didn't tell me if they are really
  separating.'

    The question word **ali** is frequently re-duced to a shorter **a** or is omitted in conversa-tion (but not in formal literary texts):

Imáte ávto?
  'Do you have a car?'
A razúmete slovénsko?
  'Do you understand Slovene?'
Je Ánica tó védela?
  'Did Anica know this?'

    In questions to which the answer is 'yes' or 'no' such as the preceding a special sentence rising intonation is used in speech. Further, the omission of the word **ali** implies the continuation of an ongoing conversation, i.e.

ali may be dropped at any point in a conversation once the general **theme** or subject matter under discussion has already been established. Example: **Se je Rájko rés poróčil?** 'Did Rajko really get married?' Here it is apparent that the topic of Rajko's marriage has already been raised (also implied in the word **res**).

The presence of **clitics**, i.e. the short forms of pronouns (see pp. 47-49) and **auxiliaries** (forms of the verb **bíti** 'to be' used with the descriptive participle in -l for the past and future tenses, see p. 78-80), in a sentence or clause is rigidly defined (although not always so rigidly followed in conversation). They **must** occupy the second position in declarative sentences and questions, and they themselves follow an accepted order. The list below provides a guide to the prescribed word order for sentences which contain clitics and/or auxiliaries:

1. introductory (head) word / constituent
   (a) The introductory word, normally stressed, may be an independent word (see p. 120) OR constituent such as a phrase or even an entire clause (see p. 127).
   (b) Alternatively the introductory word may be **ali**, the particle **naj** or a conjunction such as **da, in** or **če**.
2. (a) forms of the present tense of the verb **bíti** 'to be' used as past tense auxiliaries, **except for je**:
       sem, si, sva, sta, smo, ste, so
   (b) the word **bi** (conditional particle)
3. the reflexive pronouns **se** and **si**
4. the dative enclitic pronouns: **mi, ti, mu, ji, nama, vama, jima, nam, vam, jim**
5. the accusative enclitic pronouns: **me, te, ga, jo, naju, vaju, ju, nas, vas, jih**
6. the genitive enclitic pronouns: **me, te, ga, je, naju, vaju, ju, nas, vas, jih**
7. (a) forms of the future tense of the verb **bíti** 'to be' used as future tense auxiliaries: **bom, boš, bo, bova, bosta, bomo, boste, bodo**
       OR

(b) the 3rd person singular present tense
of the verb **bíti** 'to be': je
NOTE: Students of Slovene with a knowledge of
Serbo-Croatian should take note of the significant difference in clitic word order in the
two languages. The pattern for Serbo-Croatian
is the following:
1.) head word/constituent or the particle li
2.) auxiliaries of past, future or conditional
(except for je)
3.) dative pronoun
4.) genitive/accusative pronoun
5.) reflexive pronoun
6.) auxiliary **je**.

        Below are samples of several simple short
sentences illustrating word order with clitics
in Slovene. They may be checked against the
rules established above. They will then be fol-
lowed by a series of fuller sentences:
Dál sem mu. / Dál sem mu ga.
    'I gave it to him.'
Dála mu je. / Dála mu ga je.
    'She gave it to him.'
Prinésel sem ji. / Prinésel sem ji jo.
    'I brought it to her.'
Prinêsla mu je. / Prinêsla mu jo je.
    'She brought it to him.'
Ali si mu ga dál?
    'Did you give it to him.?'
Ali mi ga boš dál?
    'Will you give it to me?'
Ali bi ti ga dála?
    'Would she give it to you?'
Ali mu ga je dál?
    'Did he give it to him?'
        The descriptive participle in -l used to
form the past and future tenses with forms of
the verb **bíti** 'to be' is stressed and may appear
as the introductory (head) word (see examples
8., 9., 10. below and notes which follow) or may
follow the clitic(s) (examples 1., 2., 3., 4.,
5., 7., 15.-19.) if another word acts as the
introductory word and begins the sentence. Note

further that the negative particle **ne** normally
stands before the verb which it negates, including before the future forms of **bíti** and the
conditional particle **bi**. In such cases it counts
as part of the entire constituent (examples 11.,
17., 18., 19.). In those rare instances when **ne**
is separated from the verb it may act as the
head word of a sentence as in: **Ne se vèč báti,
ne vèč úpati**. 'Fear no more, hope no more.'
Negated auxiliary verbs of the past tense require that they cease to act as clitics. They
acquire stress and become full words in a sentence and precede the participle in -l (examples
12., 13., 14 and notes below).

     Study the list of examples below and the
notes which follow it. Each sentence begins with
an independent word [noun, pronoun, verb, adverb
(examples 1., 2., 3., 4., 5.) or the participle
in -l (examples 8., 9., 10. and final notes)] /
constituent (examples 6., 7. and notes below) or
the word **ali** (examples 20., 21., 22.). Some
sentences have clauses introduced by full words
(examples 23., 24.) or by the conjunctions **da**
and **če** (examples 25., 26., 27., 28., 29., 30.).
The final notes return to sentences with negated
auxiliaries, longer constituent phrases and
sentences which appear to deviate from the rule
concerning introductory words. Use the following
simplifed chart for reference:

INTRODUCTORY WORD/CONSTITUENT FOLLOWED BY:
1. PRESENT TENSE OF **BITI** (except **je**) or **BI**
               +
      SE/SI + DAT/ACC/GEN
           OR
2.   **SE/SI** + DAT/ACC/GEN
               +
      FUTURE OF **BITI** or **JE**
          Examples:
1. *Vsè je biló zasédeno.*
    'All the seats were taken.'
2. *Jóže mu je telefoníral.*
    'Joe called him.'
3. *Rôke so se mu začéle trésti.*
    'His hands began to shake.'

4. *Potém smo se razšlì.*
       'Then we went our separate ways.'
5. *Obkléj se je pojávil?*
       'When did he show up?'
6. *Kóliko letalíšč je v Slovéniji?*
       'How many airports are there in
        Slovenia?'
7. *Vsè tó ste vídeli?*
       'Did you see all of that?'
8. *Smejál se mi je.*
       'He was laughing at me.'
9. *Smejál sem se mu.*
       'I was laughing at him.'
10. *Kupíla mi je knjígo.*
       'She bought me a book.'
11. *Ne vídim ga.*
       'I don't see him.'
12. *Dúšan ga ni vídel.*
       'Dušan didn't see him.'
13. *Jaz je nisem vídel.*
       'I didn't see her.'
14. *Načŕt se ni posréčil.*
       'The plan did not succeed.'
15. *Jóže bo telefoníral.*
       'Joe will call'.
16. *On se vam bo smejál.*
       'He'll be laughing at you.'
17. *Dúšan ga ne bo vídel.*
       'Dušan won't see him.'
18. *Jaz je ne bom vídel.*
       'I won't be seeing her.'
19. *Takó ne bo šlò.*
       'This won't do.'
20. *Ali naj se mu opravíčim?*
       'Should I apologize to him?'
21. *Ali mi lahkó povéste...?*
       'Can you tell me....?'
22. *Ali si boš zapómnil vsè tó?*
       'Will you keep all that in mind?'
23. *Ne vém, kdo bi lahkó svétoval bolje.*
       'I don't know who could give better
        advice.'
24. *Vsè mu je dál, kàr je imél.*
       'He gave him everything that he had.'

25. *Míslim, da se je bál psà.*
    'I think that he was afraid of the
    dog.'
26. *Upam, da ga bom vídel.*
    'I hope that I shall see him.'
27. *Oprostíte, da vas še ênkrat nadlégujem.*
    'Forgive me for bothering you again.'
28. *Míslim, da je hotél stàr.*
    'I think that the hotel is old.'
29. *Olge ni domá, če se ne motím.*
    'Olga is not at home, if I'm not wrong.'
30. *Odšèl bi, če bi šlò po môjem.*
    'I'd leave if it were up to me.'

NOTE: In the following sentences the negated particle or auxiliary appears as the first element:
Ne bi me vídela.   'She wouldn't see me.'
(compare: Vídela bi me.   'She would see me.')
Nísem je vídel.   'I didn't see her.'
(compare: Vídel sem jo.   'I did see her.')
Ni se nam posréčilo, da bi ga vídeli.
    'We did not succeed in seeing him.'
NOTE: Entire phrases, clauses, or questions may
fill the role of the first constituent of a
sentence, e.g.
S tó stvarjó sem se mnógo bávil.
    'I've given a lot of thought to it.'
    [= I have occupied myself with that thing
    a lot.]
«Létos sem bilà v Ljubljáni», je rêkla.
    '"I was in Ljubljana this summer," she
    said.'
«Káj se je zgodílo?» so vprašáli.
    '"What happened?" they asked.'
«Prídem zjútraj, če bom mógel», je rékel.
    '"I'll come tomorrow if I can," he said.'
NOTE: Despite the rules established above, the
following two responses to the questions posed
begin with a clitic. That is because they are
part of an ongoing conversation. They follow the
rules established above for the use of the question word ali (pp. 124-125), and the pronoun
is implied:
Kjé je Jánez?   'Where is Janez?'
Je že prišèl!   'He's already arrived!'

Ali sì mój prijátelj?   *'Are you my friend?'*
Sèm in ostánem.   *'I am and shall so remain.'*
NOTE: In the following sentences the presence of
the clitics before the verb is possible because
each sentence has been shortened by deleting the
initial word. They are uttered with a single
stress:
   [Ali] Si ga vídel?   *'Have you seen him?'*
   [To] Se mi je smejál. *'He was laughing at me.'*
   [Compare the preceding sentence with the
   "correct" version, example 8., in the list
   of sentences above.]
NOTE: Likewise the participle in -l often precedes the auxiliary in declarative sentences:
   Dál sem mu ga.   *'I gave it to him.'*
   Bíl sem v Slovéniji.   *'I was in Slovenia.'*

      The above sentences follow the rule of
information of least and maximum significance.
One could change the emphasis in the second one
from 'in Slovenia' to 'was' by saying:
      V Slovéniji sem bíl.
[**HINT**: Try reading aloud the English sentence,
first stressing 'was' and then 'Slovenia':
      I wás in Slovénia.
The first variant in English equals the sentence
above. The second equals the Slovene sentence
ending with the words **v Slovéniji.**]
      In interrogatives, however, the auxiliary
precedes the participle in-l form (see above):
   Si bilà v Slovéniji? *'Were you in Slovenia?'*
   Ne, nísem bilà.   *'No, I wasn't.'*
   (The word **ali** is missing / implied in the
   question.)

SOME HINTS ON ENRICHING YOUR VOCABULARY

One of the most difficult problems in learning a new language is the acquisition of vocabulary. For the speaker of English the memorization and activization of new words in a Slavic language such as Slovene is no exception. They appear exotic and remote at the beginning. The following comments provide a few hints on how to recognize seemingly new words thereby expanding one's existing vocabulary.

At the beginning stages of his or her study of Slovene the learner is particularly advised to take note of word roots, **prefixes** and **suffixes**. On p. 92 it was shown how a basic verb may change meanings, sometimes radically, by the addition of a prefix. Learning to make informed guesses as to the meaning of a prefixed or suffixed word will help to increase one's vocabulary more quickly, and each newly encountered word will not need to be checked in a dictionary as a totally unknown item. Nouns, like verbs, may also add a prefix and acquire a new meaning, for example the following nouns of which contain the root **-hod** (cf. **hodíti** 'to walk'):

dohòd	*'access'*
izhòd	*'exit'*
obhòd	*'rounds' ('to make one's...')*
odhòd	*'departure'*
prihòd	*'arrival'*
razhòd	*'parting'*
shòd	*'meeting'/'assembly'*
vhòd	*'entrance'*
zahòd	*'west'/'sundown'*

Similarly, Slovene is rich in suffixes. Acquiring a working knowledge of them will help to expand one's vocabulary. For example, the word **bràt** 'brother' is presented below with a number of different suffixes added to it:

brátec	*'little brother'*
brátranec	*'cousin'*
brátenje	*'fraternizing'*
brátov	*'brother's'*
brátovski	*'brotherly'*

> *brátski*   'fraternal'
> *brátstvo*   'brotherhood'
> *brátovščina* 'fellowship'
> **and compounds such as:**
> *bratomòr*   'fratricide'
> *bratomóren* 'fratricidal'

The word **knjíga** 'book' has many derivative forms:

> *knjigárna*   'bookshop'
> *knjížen/knjižéven* 'literary'
> *knjižévnost*   'literature'
> *knjižévnik*   'author'
> *knjižévnica*   '(female) author'
> *knjížnica*   'library'
> *knjížničar*   'librarian'
> *knjížničarstvo*   'librarianship'

and compounds such as:

> *knjigotŕštvo*   'bookselling'
> *knjigotŕžec*   'bookseller'
> *knjigovéštvo*   'bookbinding'
> *knjigovéz*   'bookbinder'
> *knjigovéznica*   'book bindery'
> *knjigovódja*   'accountant'
> *knjigovódstvo*   'bookkeeping'

In the preceding lists of words many of the suffixes most frequently found in Slovene appeared, e.g. -stvo, -(n)ost, -ščina, which are used to form nouns of a more abstract nature from adjectives and other nouns (compare them to English nouns with the suffixes -ness, -hood, -kind, -ity and -ship). Additional words:

> *bogástvo* 〈 *bogàt* 'rich' = 'wealth'
> *človéštvo* 〈 *člôvek* 'rich' = 'mankind'
> *tóčnost* 〈 *tóčen* 'precise' = 'preciseness'
> *dvoúmnost* 〈 *dvá* 'two'+*úm* 'sense'='ambiguity'
> *soséščina* 〈 *sósed* 'neighbor'='neighborhood'
> *míloščina* 〈 *míl* 'gentle' = 'charity'

The suffix **-ina** implies a grouping of some sort as in the word **skupína** 'group' (cf. the adverb **skúpaj** 'together'). Less common are the abstract suffixes **-ota** and **-oba** as in **toplôta** 'warmth' from **tópel** 'warm' and **zlôba** 'malice' from **zlò** 'evil'.

Adjectives formed by the addition of the suffixes **-ski**, as well as **-ov/-ev** and **-ovski** to nouns ending in a consonant also appeared. To the preceding list the suffix **-in**, used to derive adjectives from nouns ending in **-a**, such as **sêstra** 'sister' : **sêstrin** 'sister's', may be added. The suffixes **-ov** and **-in** are used with masculine and feminine nouns (including proper names) respectively to form possessives (see also note 2. (b) on p. 38). The suffix **-čji** often fills the same role for animals: **máčji** 'cat's' < **máčka** 'cat'. The suffix **-en** is used frequently to derive adjectives from nouns, e.g. **glásben** 'musical' < **glásba** 'music', and the suffix **-nji** may often create an adjective from an adverb such as **sedánji** 'present'/'current' < **sedáj** 'now'.

Professions and roles which people occupy in life are designated, among others, by the suffixes **-ec**, **-nik**, **-telj**, and **-tor**. Feminine nouns may be formed from them by the addition of the suffixes **-ka**, **-ica** and **-nica**:

gréš + nik/nica	*'male/female sinner'*
diréktor/ica	*'male/female director'*
prijá + telj/teljica	*'male/female friend'*
Slovén + ec/ka	*'male/female Slovene'*

Among Slovene suffixes are a number which serve to create diminuitives from other nouns. The most common include **-ca**, **-ica** and **-ka** from nouns belonging to feminine declensions, **-ec**, **-ek** and **-ič** for masculine declension nouns and **-ece** for neuter declension nouns:

róža/róžica	*'rose'/'small rose'*
têta/têtka	*'aunt'/'auntie'*
Ána/Ánica	*'Ann'/'Annie'*
stvár/stvárca	*'thing'/'little thing'*
fànt/fántek/fantìč	*'boy'/'little boy'*
vŕt/vŕtec	*'garden'/'little garden'*
mésto/méstece	*'town'/'small town'*

Slovene shares two cognate international suffixes with English, i.e. **-ist**, as in **slavíst** 'Slavist' and **-izem** (note spelling) as in **liberalízem** 'liberalism'.

Two additional suffixes which designate a place or locale where actions take place merit special attention. The first of these is **-arna**, as in the word **knjigárna** above. The other one is **-išče** as in **gledališče** 'theater' (the place where one goes 'to watch'/'to look' **glédati**).

Also commonly used and easy to recognize are **verbal nouns (gerunds)**. Although they belong to the category of verbs, they are fully declined like Class I neuter nouns. They are formed from the past passive participle by the addition of the suffix -je to the -n or -t. (Refer to the formation of past passive adjectival participles on pp. 87-89, including the rules applicable to consonant alternations):

čístiti 'to clean' ~ *čiščénje* 'cleansing'
díhati 'to breathe' ~ *díhanje*   'breathing'
goréti 'to burn'   ~ *gorênje*   'burning'
govoríti 'to talk' ~ *govorjénje* 'talking'
hraníti 'to feed'   ~ *hránjenje* 'feeding'
potováti 'to travel'~ *potovánje* 'travelling'
spáti 'to sleep'   ~ *spánje*   'sleep'
vprášati 'to ask'   ~ *vprašánje* 'question'
bíti 'to beat'   ~ *bítje*   'beating'
gréti 'to warm'   ~ *grétje*   'heating'
péti 'to sing'   ~ *pétje*   'singing'

In the final group below all of the words contain the root **del-**. This root carries the basic meaning of 'work'. As one gains greater fluency in Slovene, it will become easier to make intelligent guesses as to the meaning of words, once having acquired a basic inventory of roots / base words.

délo   'work'
délati   'to work'
délavec   'worker'
délaven   'busy'('at work')/'industrious'
délavka   'working woman'
delávnica   'workroom'
délavnik   'work day'
délavnost   'diligence'
délavski   'workers' '
délavstvo   'working class'
delazmóžen 'able to work'

delodajálec	*'employer' ('giver of work')*
delojemálec	*'employee'('one who accepts work')*
delokróg	*'sphere (circle) of action'*
delomŕzen	*'lazy' ('unwilling to work')*
delopúst	*'time off from work' (closing time before holidays/weekends)*
delovánje	*'working', 'activity'*
delováti	*'to be in operation'*
déloven	*'working' (as in work day)*
delovódja	*'foreman'('work leader')*

GRAMMATICAL TERMINOLOGY

The following is a list in English and Slovene of grammatical terms used in this reference grammar.

alphabet   abecéda
sound   glás
       vowel   samoglásnik
       length   dolžína
       long   dólg
       short   krátek
       stress   poudárek
       stressed   poudárjen
       accent   naglàs
       open   odpŕt (širòk)
       closed   zapŕt (ózek)
       consonant   soglásnik
       voiced   zvenèč
       voiceless   nezvenèč
       change   spremémba
       alternation
         due to   mehčánje
       softening
syllable   zlòg

GENERAL GRAMMATICAL TERMINOLOGY

gender   spòl
       masculine   môški
       neuter   srédnji
       feminine   žénski
root   korén
stem   osnóva
form   oblíka
ending   obrazílo
       zero ending   núlto obrazílo
declension   sklanjátev
case   sklòn
       nominative   imenoválnik
       accusative   tožílnik
       genitive   rodílnik
       dative   dajálnik
       locative   méstnik
       instrumental   oródnik
number   števílo

	singular	ednína
	dual	dvojína
	plural	množína
noun	samostálnik	
	animate	žív
	inanimate	nežív
adjective	pridévnik	
	definite	dolóčni
	indefinite	nèdolóčni
	gradation	stopnjevánje
	positive	osnóvnik
	comparative	primérnik
	superlative	preséžnik
adverb	prislòv	
pronoun	zaímek	
	personal	osébni
	possessive	svojílni
	demonstrative	kazálni
	interrogative	vprašálni
	relative	ozirálni
	indefinite	nèdolóčni
	reflexive	povrátni
numeral	štévnik	
	cardinal	glávni
	ordinal	vrstílni
	collective	ločílni
	multiplicative	množílni
preposition	prêdlog	
conjunction	véznik	
verb	glágol	
	conjugation	spregátev
	aspect	víd
	imperfective	nèdovŕšni
	perfective	dovŕšni
	transitive	prehódni
	intransitive	nèprehódni
	verb of motion	glágol premíkanja
	auxiliary	pomóžni
	reflexive	povrátni
	prefix	predpóna
	suffix	pripóna
	infinitive	nèdolóčnik
	supine	namenílnik
	tense	čàs
	present	sedánji

```
          past           pretêkli
          future         prihódnji
          person         oséba
          first          pŕva
          second         drúga
          third          trétja
          participle     deléžnik
          descriptive                   opísni(na-l)
          present adverbial             na -e
          past adverbial                na -(v)ši
          present adjectival            na -č
          past passive adjectival na -n, -t
          mood           naklòn
          indicative     povédni
          voice          način
          active         tvórni (áktiv)
          middle         srédnji
          =(reflexive)   (povrátni/médij)
          passive        tŕpni (pásiv)
          imperative     velélnik
          optative       želélnik
          conditional    pogójnik
sentence  stávek
          simple         prôsti
          complex        zložêni
          subject        osébek
          object         prêdmet
          declarative    izjávni
          interrogative  vprašálni
          dependent      odvísni
          independent    samostójni/glávni

punctuation    ločíla
          period             píka
          question mark      vprašáj
          comma              vêjica
          exclamation mark klicáj
          colon              dvópíčje
          semi-colon         pòdpíčje
          dash               pomišljáj
          hyphen             vezáj
          parentheses        oklepáj
          quotation marks    narekováj
```

WORD INDEX

The index which follows includes words used throughout the text to illustrate grammatical and lexical points, including those used in sample declensions and conjugations. Words discussed in notes which constitute exceptional forms are likewise included. Individual vocabulary items used in sentences have not been included except for those introduced to emphasize a grammatical point. Finally, for the most part those words which are presented in list form throughout the text have been excluded from the word index, and the reader should refer to them separately. They include items such as: voiced and voiceless consonants (pp. 19-20); consonant alternations (pp. 20-21); comparative forms of adjectives (pp. 40-43); comparative forms of adverbs (p. 44); pronouns (pp. 47-53); cardinal and ordinal numerals (pp. 54-55); prepositions (pp. 60-64); imperative verbs (pp. 80-82); the several participles (pp. 84-89); verbal prefixes and prefixed verbs (pp. 91-92); pairs of imperfective and perfective verbs (pp. 92-93); verbs with the reflexive pronouns se/si (pp. 96-98); verbal stress (pp. 99-101); use of the dual (pp. 102-103); verbs of motion (p. 111); telling time (pp. 114-115); names of the days of the week, months, divisions of the day and seasons (pp. 118-119); word formation (pp. 131-135); grammatical terminology in English and Slovene (pp. 136-138).

SUBJECT INDEX

145

BIBLIOGRAPHY

The books listed below under **Works Consulted** have been extremely useful in writing this work, in particular those by Bajec et al., Kopčavar, Lencek and Toporišič. They provided critical information on grammatical forms as well as examples of usage. Likewise, the Grad dictionaries proved invaluable. Many of the examples used throughout the text were borrowed from the preceding works.

WORKS CONSULTED

Anton Bajec, Rudolf Kolarič & Mirko Rupel.
  Slovenska slovnica. Expan. ed. Ljubljana:
  Državna založba Slovenije, 1973.
Charles E. Bidwell. *Outline of Slovenian Morphology*. Pittsburgh, PA: University of
  Pittsburgh, Center for International Studies,
  1969.
Reginald G. A. de Bray. *Guide to the Slavonic
  Languages*. 3rd rev.ed. Part I, *Guide to
  the South Slavonic Languages*. Columbus, OH:
  Slavica, 1980.
Ileana & Cene Kopčavar. *Jezikovna vadnica*.
  Ljubljana: Državna založba Slovenije, 1977.
Rado L. Lencek. *The Structure and History of
  the Slovene Language*. Columbus, OH:
  Slavica, 1982.
Rado L. Lencek. *The Verb Pattern of Contemporary Slovene with an Attempt at a Generative
  Description of the Slovene Verb by Horace G.
  Lunt*. Wiesbaden: Harrasowitz, 1966.
Tine Logar. *Slovenska narečja: Besedila*.
  Ljubljana: Mladinska knjiga, 1975.
Elfriede Mader. *Rücklaüfiges Wörterbuch des
  slowenischen*. Klagenfurt: Klagenfurter
  Beiträge zur Sprachwissenshaft. Slawistische
  Reihe 5, 1981.
Jože Toporišič. *Slovenska slovnica*. 2nd ed.
  Maribor: Založba Obzorja, 1984.
Claude Vincenot. *Essai de grammaire slovène*.
  Ljubljana: Mladinska knjiga, 1975.

France Žagar. *Slovenska slovnica in jezikovna vadnica*. Maribor: Založba Obzorja, 1988.

TEXTBOOKS OF SLOVENE

Ema Andoljšek, Ludvik Jevšenak & Tomo Korošec. *Povejmo slovensko*. Ljubljana: Državna za- ložba Slovenije, 1973.

anon. *Slovenian Non-Resident Language Re- fresher Course: 210 Hour Course*. (7 vols.) Monterey, CA: Army Language School, 1961–63. (accompanying recordings available)

Milena Gobetz & Breda Loncar. *Slovenian Langu- age Manual: Učbenik slovenskega jezika*. 2 vols. Willoughby Hills, OH: Slovenian Research Center, 1976 & 1977.

Miran Hladnik & Toussaint Hočevar. *Slovene for Travellers. Slovenščina za popotnike*. (with two accompanying casettes) Ljubljana: Center za ekonomsko in turistično propagando, 1988.

Franc Jakopin. *Slovene for You. Učbenik slo- venskega jezika*. Ljubljana: Slovenska izseljenska matica, 1962.

Hermina Jug-Kranjec. *Slovenščina za tujce*. Ljubljana: Seminar slovenskega jezika, literature in kulture. 5th and expan. ed., 1987.

Janko Jurančič. *Slovenački (slovenski) jezik: Gramatika slovenačkoga (slovenskog) jezika za Hrvate i Srbe*. 2nd rev. ed. Ljubljana: Državna založba Slovenije, 1971.

Martina Križaj-Otar. *Učimo se slovenščino*. In 4 parts. Ljubljana: Seminar slovenskega jezika, literature in kulture, 1987.

Manja Škrubej, ed., *Slovenščina. Slovene. A Self-Study Course*. 3 vols. (with twelve accompanying casettes) [Based on *Povejmo slovensko* by E. Andoljšek *et al*., see above], Ljubljana: RTV Ljubljana, 1983.

G. O. Svane. *Grammatik der slowenischen Schriftsprache*. Copenhagen: Rosenkilde and Bagger, 1958.

Jože Toporišič. *Zakaj ne po slovensko. Slovene
by Direct Method.* (with six accompanying
records) Ljubljana: Slovenska izseljenska
matica, 1969.

DICTIONARIES

Anton Bajec, et al., eds. *Slovenski pravopis.*
rev. ed. Ljubljana: Slovenska akademija
znanosti in umetnosti, 1962.
_____. *Slovar slovenskega knjižnega jezika.*
4 vols. (A-S). Ljubljana: Slovenska akademija
znanosti in umetnosti, 1970-1985.
Anton Grad. *The Great Slovene-English Dictionary.*
Veliki slovensko-angleški slovar. Ljubljana:
Državna založba Slovenije, 1982.
Anton Grad, Ružena Skerlj & Nada Vitorovič.
*The Great English-Slovene Dictionary. Veliki
angleško-slovenski slovar.* Ljubljana: Državna
založba Slovenije, 1978.
Daša Komac & Ružena Skerlj. *Angleško-slovenski
in slovensko-angleški slovar. English-Slovene
and Slovene-English Dictionary.* 7th ed.
Ljubljana: Cankarjeva založba, 1981.
Janko Kotnik. *Slovene-English Dictionary. Sloven-
sko-angleški slovar.* 8th rev. ed. Ljubljana:
Državna založba, 1978.
Joseph Paternost. *Slovenian-English Glossary of
Linguistic Terms.* University Park, PA: Penn-
sylvania State University, Department of
Slavic Languages, 1966.
Maks Pleteršnik. *Slovensko-nemški slovar.*
2 vols. Ljubljana, 1894-1895. [Reprint by
Cankarjeva založba, Ljubljana, 1974.]

Other Books From Slavica

Ronelle Alexander: *The Structure of Vasko Popa's Poetry*.

American Contributions to the Tenth International Congress of Slavists, Sofia, September, 1988, Linguistics, ed. **Alexander M. Schenker**.

American Contributions to the Ninth International Congress of Slavists (Kiev 1983) Vol. 1: Linguistics, ed. **Michael S. Flier**.

American Contributions to the Eighth International Congress of Slavists, Vol 1: Linguistics and Poetics, ed. **Henrik Birnbaum**.

Howard I. Aronson: *Georgian: A Reading Grammar*.

Henrik Birnbaum & Thomas Eekman, eds.: *Fiction and Drama in Eastern and Southeastern Europe: Evolution and Experiment in the Postwar Period*.

Marianna D. Birnbaum: *Humanists in a Shattered World: Croatian and Hungarian Latinity in the Sixteenth Century*.

F. J. Bister and Herbert Kuhner, eds.: *Carinthian Slovenian Poetry*.

Ralph Bogert: *The Writer as Naysayer Miroslav Krleža and the Aesthetic of Interwar Central Europe*.

Terence R. Carlton: *Introduction to the Phonological History of the Slavic Languages*.

Henry R. Cooper, Jr. ed.: *Papers in Slovene Studies 1978*.

Andrew R. Corin: *The New York Missal: A Paleographic and Phonetic Analysis*.

Dorothy Disterheft: *The Syntactic Development of the Infinitive in Indo-European*.

Per Durst-Andersen: *Mental Grammar Russian Aspect and Related Issues*.

M. J. Elson: *Macedonian Verbal Morphology A Structural Analysis*.

M. S. Flier and R. D. Brecht, eds.: *Issues in Russian Morphosyntax*.

John M. Foley, ed.: *Oral Traditional Literature A Festschrift for Albert Bates Lord*.

John Miles Foley, ed.: *Comparative Research on Oral Traditions: A Memorial for Milman Parry*.

Other Books From Slavica

Zbigniew Gołąb: *The Origin of the Slavs A Linguist's View*.

Charles E. Gribble: *Reading Bulgarian Through Russian*.

Charles E. Gribble: *Russian Root List with a Sketch of Word Formation*.

Charles E. Gribble: *A Short Dictionary of 18th-Century Russian/ Словарик Русского Языка 18-го Века*.

Morris Halle, ed.: *Roman Jakobson: What He Taught Us*.

Morris Halle, Krystyna Pomorska, Elena Semeka-Pankratov, and Boris Uspenskij, eds.: *Semiotics and the History of Culture In Honor of Jurij Lotman Studies in Russian*.

William S. Hamilton: *Introduction to Russian Phonology and Word Structure*.

Michael Heim: *Contemporary Czech*.

Michael Heim, Z. Meyerstein, and Dean Worth: *Readings in Czech*.

Warren H. Held, Jr., William R. Schmalstieg, and Janet E. Gertz: *Beginning Hittite*.

Peter Hill: *The Dialect of Gorno Kalenik*.

M. Hubenova & others: *A Course in Modern Bulgarian*.

Martin E. Huld: *Basic Albanian Etymologies*.

Roman Jakobson: *Brain and Language*

Emily R. Klenin: *Animacy in Russian: A New Interpretation*.

Mark Kulikowski: *A Bibliography of Slavic Mythology*.

Richard L. Leed, Alexander D. Nakhimovsky, and Alice S. Nakhimovsky: *Beginning Russian, Second Revised Edition*.

Richard L. Leed and Slava Paperno: *5000 Russian Words With All Their Inflected Forms: A Russian-English Dictionary*.

Edgar H. Lehrman: *A Handbook to Eighty-Six of Chekhov's Stories in Russian*.

Gail Lenhoff: *The Martyred Princes Boris and Gleb: A Social-Cultural Study of the Cult and the Texts*.

Other Books From Slavica

Maurice I. Levin: *Russian Declension and Conjugation: A Structural Description with Exercises.*

Yvonne R. Lockwood: *Text and Context Folksong in a Bosnian Muslim Village.*

Paul Macura: *Russian-English Botanical Dictionary.*

Robert Mann: *Lances Sing: A Study of the Igor Tale.*

Stephen Marder: *A Supplementary Russian-English Dictionary.*

V. Markov and **D. S. Worth**, eds.: *From Los Angeles to Kiev Papers on the Occasion of the Ninth International Congress of Slavists.*

Mateja Matejić and **Dragan Milivojević:** *An Anthology of Medieval Serbian Literature in English.*

Gordon M. Messing: *A Glossary of Greek Romany As Spoken in Agia Varvara (Athens).*

Vasa D. Mihailovich and **Mateja Matejic:** *A Comprehensive Bibliography of Yugoslav Literature in English, 1593-1980.*

Vasa D. Mihailovich: *First Supplement to* A Comprehensive Bibliography of Yugoslav Literature in English *1981-1985.*

Vasa D. Mihailovich: *Second Supplement to* A Comprehensive Bibliography of Yugoslav Literature in English *1981-1985.*

Dragan Milivojević and **Vasa D. Mihailovich:** *A Bibliography of Yugoslav Linguistics in English 1900-1980.*

Edward Możejko: *Yordan Yovkov.*

Alexander D. Nakhimovsky and Richard L. Leed: *Advanced Russian, Second Edition, Revised.*

T. Pachmuss: *Russian Literature in the Baltic between the World Wars.*

Lora Paperno: *Getting Around Town in Russian: Situational Dialogs*, English translation and photographs by **Richard D. Sylvester.**

Slava Paperno, Alexander D. Nakhimovsky, Alice S. Nakhimovsky, and Richard L. Leed: *Intermediate Russian: The Twelve Chairs.*

Jan L. Perkowski: *The Darkling A Treatise on Slavic Vampirism.*

Leonard A. Polakiewicz: *Supplemental Materials for First Year Polish.*

Other Books From Slavica

Gilbert C. Rappaport: *Grammatical Function and Syntactic Structure: The Adverbial Participle of Russian.*

Catherine Rudin: *Aspects of Bulgarian Syntax: Complementizers and WH Constructions.*

William R. Schmalstieg: *Introduction to Old Church Slavic.*

William R. Schmalstieg: *A Lithuanian Historical Syntax.*

P. Seyffert: *Soviet Literary Structuralism: Background Debate Issues.*

Kot K. Shangriladze and **Erica W. Townsend,** eds: *Papers for the V. Congress of Southeast European Studies (Belgrade, September 1984).*

Theofanis G. Stavrou and **Peter R. Weisensel:** *Russian Travelers to the Christian East from the Twelfth to the Twentieth Century.*

G. Stone and **D. S. Worth,** eds.: *The Formation of the Slavonic Literary Languages, Proceedings of a Conference Held in Memory of Robert Auty and Anne Pennington at Oxford 6-11 July 1981.*

Rudolph M. Susel, ed.: *Papers in Slovene Studies 1977.*

Roland Sussex and **J. C. Eade,** eds.: *Culture and Nationalism in Nineteenth-Century Eastern Europe.*

Oscar E. Swan and **Sylvia Gálová-Lorinc:** *Beginning Slovak.*

Oscar E. Swan: *First Year Polish.*

Oscar E. Swan: *Intermediate Polish.*

Charles E. Townsend: *Continuing With Russian.*

Charles E. Townsend: *Czech Through Russian.*

Charles E. Townsend: *A Description of Spoken Prague Czech.*

Charles E. Townsend: *Russian Word Formation.*

Boryana Velcheva: *Proto-Slavic and Old Bulgarian Sound Changes.*

Dean S. Worth: *Origins of Russian Grammar Notes on the state of Russian philology before the advent of printed grammars.*

Yordan Yovkov: *The Inn at Antimovo* and *Legends of Stara Planina*, translated from Bulgarian by John Burnip.